You're Not Who You Think You Are

You're Not Who You Think You Are

A Breakthrough Guide to Discovering the Authentic You

■■■

Albert Clayton Gaulden

ATRIA BOOKS

New York   London   Toronto   Sydney

A Division of Simon & Schuster, Inc.
1230 Avenue of the Americas
New York, NY 10020

First Atria Books hardcover edition December 2008

ATRIA BOOKS and colophon are trademarks of Simon & Schuster, Inc.

For information about special discounts for bulk purchases, please contact
Simon & Schuster Special Sales at 1-800-456-6798 or
business@simonandschuster.com.

Designed by C. Linda Dingler

Manufactured in the United States of America

10 9 8 7 6 5 4 3 2 1

Library of Congress Cataloging-in-Publication Data

Gaulden, Albert Clayton.
   You're not who you think you are / by Albert Clayton
Gaulden.— Rev. ed.
      p. cm.
   1. Spiritual life. 2. Self-perception—Religious aspects.
3. Self-actualization (Psychology)—Religious aspects. I. Title.

   BL624.G367 2008
   204'.4—dc22   2007052593

ISBN-13: 978-1-4165-8376-9
ISBN-10:   1-4165-8376-9

To Scott Carney
and the Bells

Contents

FOREWORD
by James Redfield   ix

PROLOGUE:
Discovering Albert   1

CHAPTER 1:
Reconnecting to the Light   21

CHAPTER 2:
Stage One—Converting the Ego   45

CHAPTER 3:
Stage Two—Answering the Question,
"God or No God?"   59

CHAPTER 4:
Stage Three—Out of the Darkness
and Into the Light   73

Contents

CHAPTER 5:

Stage Four—Karmic Mirrors   101

CHAPTER 6:

Stage Five—You're Not Who You Think You Are   117

CHAPTER 7:

Stage Six—Forgive and Forget-Me-Nots   143

CHAPTER 8:

Stage Seven—Bringing Your Brother to the Light   161

CHAPTER 9:

Stage Eight—The Love Chapter: All You Need
Is Love   183

CHAPTER 10:

The End of the Journey   197

Author's Note   213

APPENDIX:

Lunar and Solar Eclipses   215

Acknowledgements   217

FOREWORD

by James Redfield

author of *The Celestine Prophecy*
and *The Tenth Insight*

I have known Albert Gaulden for more than 20 years. I first heard of him from a friend who went to see him on one of his many work trips to Alabama. "He is unblievably accurate in bringing personality issues to the surface. He also says that none of us knows who we really are," she told me over coffee one day. "He really nailed the way I was getting in my own way, blocking my potential. He showed me a more authentic person than who I was living as. You can't hide anything from Albert."

After several other people synchronistically mentioned

this astro-intuitive and transpersonal psychologist, I found myself thoroughly intrigued, so I called his booking agent and got in line, finally meeting him several days later in the Pickwick Hotel in Birmingham. It took only a few minutes for Albert's transparent personality to shine through. He is witty, mildly sarcastic, and an absolutely hilarious storyteller. And he is totally serious about what he does with his clients.

Quickly disposing of the initial banter, he beckoned me to a corner couch and placed a completed astrological chart on the table between us.

"Well," he remarked, "You're quite a secretive fellow, aren't you, and in a lot of conflict?" He went on to tell me that at this time in my life, the planet Pluto was almost 90 degrees from where it was the day I was born; that Uranus, the planet of sudden change and ruler of my sixth house of work was exactly opposing my natal Uranus in Cancer, which indicates stark changes in how I make a living. Most important, he pointed out that Uranus and Saturn were conjunct in Capricorn making a square (danger signal—indicating changes that need to be made consciously in relationships) to my natal Mars in Libra. These aspects in one's natal astrological chart signal a period in which everything in a person's life that is not conducive to his higher learning and psychological growth tends to blow up and be taken away, sometimes traumatically. In Albert's language, I had been living somebody else's life—that who I really am was waiting anxiously to surface topside. I'll never forget when he laughed and said, "James, you are not who you think you are, but I know how and where we can find the real you."

I smiled at him, remaining aloof, but he was, in fact, right on target. My life was undergoing a vast reorganization. I had ended a marriage and left a job I had held for eight years.

"Ah, yes," he continued, "There's more. You're also writing something. What is it?"

"Wait a minute," I interrupted. "How did you know that?"

He pushed the chart around where I could see it. "It's right here. You've got Venus and Jupiter in Aquarius in the fifth house being activated by transit and progression."

Now I was impressed. I had started writing *The Celestine Prophecy* about six months earlier. "I want to understand how you do this," I said.

Albert laughed, and the ensuing conversation led to a trip to Sedona to go through his famous Sedona Intensive, where Albert performed his amazing gift: helping to pull into consciousness those unconscious habits and addictions that keep us from a greater life. In my case, of course, we focused on my aloofness and reluctance to commit to a single project. And his core focus was on becoming who I was born to be as opposed to how I had been living my life. With the help of Sedona herself (those magic red hills alone seem to increase the synchronicity and provide the experiences that illustrate whatever we are learning), I became aware of exactly when my indifference kicks in, why it gets in the way, and what my real self—my authentic self—feels like when I break free of this control drama.

In this environment, I was able to spend the dedicated free time to survey my life as one story—from that first placement with my early family all the way through the twists and turns of my subsequent experiences. I found hidden meaning in old relationships, misdeeds that needed rectifying, and full acknowledgment of the preparation my past seemed to have provided me. Most of all I was to connect with a sense of freedom and inspiration that comes from living one's life honestly, with as few secrets as possible.

In retrospect, I think that Albert's emphasis on addictions and unconscious habits brought home for me the wisdom of such thinkers as Norman O. Brown and Ernest Becker, who years ago explained that we humans can evolve no further until we learn to deal with our everyday compulsions—those parts of our individual lifestyles we pursue with singular intensity, and at which we resist looking because they seem to feel so good. We know now that such activities, which can be of varying degrees of destructiveness—overworking, overeating, laziness, TVing, shopping, judging, distancing, complaining, drinking, drugging, sexual addiction—are all unconsciously designed to keep us distracted, and to fend off the ego's fear of facing the great mystery that is this life. The ego fights this recognition because it senses that it must lose total control, and because it has no idea that such recognition would merely mean expanding into a higher self full of intuition and creativity and grand adventure.

In his book, Albert seeks to convey the full scope of how to look at those defects that cover-up our real selves; he has strategies that are reachable and effective in letting go of who we are not and becoming at long last authentic. In his humorous and, yes, confrontational way, he has clearly laid out the challenge facing all of us. We can talk about a coming spiritual renaissance to any degree we want, but it cannot happen until enough of us grasp that spiritual growth has a mental health component. We all have to step back and really look at the parts of our personalities that hold us back, because only then can we become who we really are—and truly move forward into a consciousness and mission that can change the world.

You're Not Who You Think You Are

Discovering Albert

Everyone needs a touchstone.

No matter how well-refined your thinking process is, you need a sounding board of sorts. I'm not simply talking about a friend who is willing to lend an ear when you're troubled, or a mentor who will preach to you about what he or she believes is the correct action for you to take.

I'm talking about someone who can impart wisdom. A person who will ask the hard questions, the ones that push you to reflect on your inner self. On your life's work. On your relationships. On your very existence. Someone who can put you in touch with what you have inside, but might not be ready to see.

I was lucky to find that touchstone in my guru, Swami Swahananda, the spiritual head of the Vedanta Society in Southern California. The first time I met Swami, I had been hired by a close friend who was a Vedantist to meet with this venerated spiritual leader to discuss his astrological birth chart. (To tell the truth, I was taken aback that someone like him would turn to someone like me.) I was humbled to do his chart for him.

Vedanta is a philosophy based on the teachings of the Vedas, ancient Hindu scriptures. Their basic instruction is that our true nature is divine. God, the Atman or Brahmin—the underlying reality—exists in each of us. Vedanta believes that all paths that lead to God are right paths—a philosophy that complements my own beliefs.

The Vedanta Society of Southern California was founded in 1929. It maintains a temple, convent, and monastery in Hollywood and Montecito, and monasteries in Trabuco Canyon and San Diego.

I didn't discover Swami was my touchstone when we first met. I was, in fact, quite the skeptic about Vedanta. After I did Swami's reading, he and I had many discussions, one of which turned to my feelings about Vedanta.

I told Swami that I didn't believe in gurus and I would never join a cult. A lot of us—myself included—often feel contempt for a person or an "ism." Of course, that is how ignorance and misinformation can choke an open-minded attitude to death.

Swami didn't decry my strong words or take insult. Instead, he said it was better for me to believe in myself. From that time I became something of a student.

Over time I opened my mind, and I learned from him that guru means teacher in Sanskrit and that Vedanta is not a cult. I researched Ramakrishna, the founder of Vedanta, who lived from 1836 to 1886. Ramakrishna is the chosen ideal for Vedantists, just as Jesus is for Christians. Swami gave me a book, *How to Know God,* which instructs the novice in the teachings of Vedanta and how to become one with the Divine within. I was hooked.

A few months later I told Swami that I wanted to become a Vedantist. He became my teacher—an idea to which I might have said, "When hell freezes over!" upon our first introduction.

At my initiation, he gave me a Sanskrit name, Ramapriya, which means beloved of God, not as an alias to conceal my identity but to celebrate my spiritual rebirth. Only he, nuns from the Sarada Convent, and other devotees call me by that name.

This book is not a promotion for Vedanta, nor will I preach to you. But I do wish to open your eyes beyond conventional wisdom about organized religion, spirituality, and the divine within. I want to introduce you to the parts of yourself that you've buried—parts that you may not believe exist.

We're living in a world filled with powder-puff spirituality. Many spiritual authors and leaders appear to be "show dogs" or rock stars, not teachers with a clear and conscious message. Rather, the messenger has become the centerpiece of his work. Instead of deep introspection, we hear feel-good philosophies in sound bites and snippets on talk shows. Rather than paths that require commitment and steps to psychic change, isms and pop psychology are being embraced by a lot of seekers who pick it up and then throw it down when the next spiritual fad crops up. I will not treat you, my reader, as a member of a kindergarten class, but as an independent thinker who can use this book to explore what's inside of you.

This exploration, these lessons, will come in a series of "stages," inspired by William Shakespeare, a master metaphysician who insinuated everything we ever need to know about the human condition in his plays. In *As You like It*, he wrote:

All the world's a stage,
And all the men and women merely players:
They have their exits and their entrances;
And one man in his time plays many parts,
His acts being seven ages.

Who among us knew when we were kids in class struggling to glean meaning from Mr. Shakespeare's heavy-laden text that he was uncovering our return to truth and selfhood with his words and occult messages? Who among us knew that *The Merchant of Venice* was about looking at greed and selfishness and debaucheries within ourselves—during past lives or the present one— to see the Shylock mirror image of our own tarnished soul? All of the bard's plays are reflections for all of us to be able to see ourselves as others see us and as we need to see ourselves—and to realize how badly we need to change to become true to us and others.

Before you join me on this journey of stages, understand the place from which I came.

THE OLD ALBERT

My early life was not picture perfect and the concept of God was confusing to me.

My parents divorced when I was nine years old. My father was a womanizing drunk who married six times. My mother was a martyr who worked to raise six children. She was sober, God-fearing, and she always paid her bills on time

I grew up with three sisters and two brothers, none of whom would take a drink as adults. I, on the other hand, took after my dad. The Gaulden bloodline indicated that

I would be an alcoholic like my father and his father—I am a ninth-generation drunk.

When I was a child, I desperately wanted to know God. Church music and Bible stories excited me. I took lots of retreats to the mountains and the beach. One question in particular nagged at me: "If there is a God, why do I have club feet?"

Although I didn't like my club feet, the one benefit I enjoyed from them was being coddled and fussed over by doctors and nurses at Duke Hospital on and off, from the time I was born until age three. When I went home to my family, two brothers, three sisters, and bickering parents, I wanted to go back to the hospital. I wanted my nurses and my doctors. I didn't like my brothers and sisters or my parents.

I was raised a Baptist, and I was baptized, but I never believed. As a little boy, I heard voices and I saw what others couldn't. I knew what others didn't, but it didn't coincide with the religion my family wanted me to be a part of. No one was there to listen to my questions, and there was no one I could trust to tell what I saw and what I knew. So I did what I was told to do, and I believed what I was told to believe.

My Baptist minister told me I would be a minister, and I always did as I was told. I became a ministerial student and was a pastor in rural South Alabama churches, but I did not believe in Jesus as my Lord and Savior, and

I did not believe that Jesus could get me in or keep me out of Heaven. I wasn't towing the line, but it was my secret.

Alcohol eventually helped me become defiant enough to excommunicate myself from traditional religion. It also created a haze through which I could shield myself from my doubts about God.

I needed to tear my world apart so God could help it fall back into place. Being dead broke and down and out beat living a lie, until I decided to stop burying the real me with addictions and compulsions.

I found God out of desperation when I got sober. I prayed and meditated, and I intuited that God loved me. I felt He cared for me. I struggled, but learned to listen to the God within me. I began the practice of yoga—the spiritual discipline and techniques of meditation that enabled me to achieve knowledge of God. I instructed myself to quietude every day at a set time. God touched me and he opened my heart.

God had been a fly in the ointment when I first got sober. The aphorism, "To know God is to know yourself," started me exploring deep-tissue issues I had about God. My feelings turned out to be resentment against church leadership, and not a disdain for God.

Many sects and spiritual leaders use control tactics to make followers dependent on them. It is dangerous and manipulative for an organization or leader to control another person's life, telling him how to pray and what to believe, and taking away his freedom to make mistakes along the way.

I had always looked everywhere outside myself for solutions. But I found that God is within, and the role of the God within is to love and guide us when we will allow it. To know God is to know yourself, and you don't need an organized religion to find a higher power.

UNDERSTANDING ALBERT

I'm a troublemaker. I always questioned everything—believed nothing—and was suspect of everybody's motives, especially my parents, preachers, and politicians. They all had too many agendas and we all had too much blind faith. I searched high and low, read, researched everything I could get my eyes on—manuscripts, books, documents, audio tapes, and videos—and learned to pay attention to my inner voice even when I didn't know it existed. The earthly world around me was illusion; within me I found reality. I came to refer to Earth as "here" and the real world (which Christians call Heaven), "there."

Nothing in my life made sense until I understood the concept of karma; that is, "We get what we deserve." We are born, we live, we die, and then we start the process all over again. We live life after life until we clean up—clear up—our souls and become as we were initially created to be. Why would God create one person beautiful or handsome, brilliant, rich, and privileged and another ugly, stupid, and dirt poor? Why would someone be born a woman and never come back to experience being a man? Why would a child be born in Darfur with absolutely nothing, while in America even the poorest of us live in relative comfort? All of life only makes sense if we have to experience everything and everybody to pay for the things we have done to harm others. In one life we reign as king and then we reincarnate as a pauper. Again and again and again. We create the life we deserve when we let go of the world of illusion—the "un-us" world—and become clearly who we really are.

The master plan of recycling lives was devised at the beginning of time and the innate knowledge of it was buried within the subconscious of each of us. The stranglehold the Church has on the masses oftentimes keeps karma and reincarnation in the voodoo and hocus-pocus department of the library.

Karma is a magical kingdom of self-discovery, and it explains who I am. Karma knows I have done things in past lives and it knows what I am doing in this life. Karma shows me what I need to do to become real and true to my creation, what I need to change to make up for the misdeeds of my past lives. The Bombay-born Jesuit priest and psychotherapist, Anthony de Mello, was wont to say that "people are asleep. They are born asleep. They live asleep. They marry in their sleep and breed children in their sleep. They die in their sleep without ever waking up." This idea helps explain what karma is to me. I have woken up to discover that passivity through millennia got me into a lot of trouble. I must face my mistakes, face the false selves I have been and the false lives I have lived. In order to resolve my mistakes, I must face them all. Buddha's simple message is "Wake up!"

Western thought is corseted by religions, each of which has its agenda, one that does not allow us to self-legislate who we are, how to pray, or what ism or doctrine to follow. Religion has stood in its bully pulpit, defying us to transgress into that inner world where we can find ourselves. Eastern ideas are founded upon karma and reincarnation: refine the soul by finding what separates us from the Divine, and become transformed by admitting our mistakes and reforming. Prayer and meditation abet the return to our true self. In Eastern consciousness these topics are as accepted as breathing. In Western tradition leaders use fear and manipulation and control to denigrate these notions as folly.

TODAY'S ALBERT

Today, I am an astro-intuitive and counselor, mixing the principles of astrology with Jungian psychology and my sixth sense. I refer to myself as Charon, after the mythological boatman who ferried souls of the dead across the River Styx to eternal life. My assignment is to lovingly escort the troubled but courageous men and women who seek my counsel out of the darkness and into the light. This clearing process is a method of dying to the old way of life and being reborn as an authentic human being.

I do my work through the Sedona Intensive. Our five-day program began in 1982 in Sedona, Arizona. Locals who immerse themselves in metaphysical superstition say the powerful alchemical properties within Sedona's vortices are the reason our clients find a way to change themselves. This may be partially true. Perhaps some special otherworldly properties within this valley of reddish-brown carvings affect our energy bodies, and we begin to experience "wow" and "aha" phenomena. Whatever the catalyst, before the week is over, all Sedona Intensive clients go through an epiphany of transcendence: They eliminate tons and lifetimes of painful, terrifying skeletons from their closets.

I seek to see what's going on in a client's life and why he's coming to work with us at the time that he does. Before someone is accepted as a candidate, he must have a telephone astro-intuitive session with me. The birth chart gives me a good idea of how likely an individual is to respond to our program. Astrology provides accurate insights into character, assets, liabilities, and windows of opportunity for momentous things to happen in one's life. I am also adept at deciphering voice imprint. As the client speaks, I get thought impressions from the resonance of his or her voice. Helping heal character defects that show up in the astrological horoscopes of clients is my brand of therapy. I travel to major cities throughout the world to give seminars and consult with clients, from actors to professional athletes to Wall Street moguls to people in all sorts of professions.

I never talk astrology or do a horoscope session once the Intensive starts. Astrology is a convenient diversion to old-fashioned recovery. The client comes to recover from a hopeless state of mind and body, not to have me forecast a new lover, or whether he will win the lottery or she will move to Xanadu.

Before arriving in Sedona, our clients must complete writing assignments, so they can be ready to discuss their families, marriages, and relationships. They must also read required books, make daily journal entries, and meditate with CDs we furnish.

A client's visit includes daily twelve-step meetings. All clients, alcoholic, drug addict, or not, are required to attend these meetings because I contend that everybody's sick somewhere, and twelve steps is a great stopgap to those difficulties. Throughout the five days clients see me every day for an hour and a half, and I am in their faces—cajoling, challenging, arguing, surrendering, and crying for all to endure and conquer—shepherding them to a clear and clean space to heal.

Our unique therapy model was built on the solid rock of getting at the truth of who did what to whom, no matter how much pain the client has to endure. Clearing digs up taproots of denial and cleans away all toxins. Our method is to peel back the layers of a client's childhood and tap into his cellular memory of anger and rage. Then he must see the family for who they really are, cop an honest plea about his part in the melodrama, and then get on with his life. Acceptance that everybody is doing the best they can with what they have is a major step toward being released from shackles of the past. But the essence of our program is that God is at the heart of the process.

When I was getting sober in Long Beach, California, a toothless and unwashed longshoreman said in a meeting, "God created me to be one thing, and I was determined to be something else." When I addressed a reunion of clients who had been through the Sedona Intensive, I reminded them, "All the things we do to get our own way, to come into compliance with a faulty ego, are a separation-from-God problem. The entire week I try to escort you back to who God created you to be. You look at the mess you've made, separate what's a keeper from what has to go, write letters of anger and rage, and then forgive yourself and others."

My voice of intuition told me that as a sober man, "You must give away what you have found: help others to see the light and to take the steps to return to their real selves. As you have shed your own false disguises, you will help others remove their masks. You will guide them to face down the great egocentric deceiver and free the precious children of God buried in the rubble of their destructive actions."

ALBERT'S JOURNEY

"Who am I?" I asked.

My guru sat across from me. I had booked a sitting in his spartan rooms at the Vedanta Center in Hollywood.

"To know God is to know you," Swami said.

Swami listened as I complained about my career as an intuitive astrologer. Clients ask incessantly, "Where is the money?" "Will I have a new lover in my future?" "Why do bad things keep happening?" I had no more answers. I had questions for Swami.

My motive for speaking to Swami was to end my career as an astro-intuitive and instead become a custodian in the Vedanta library or become Swami's personal assistant. I was burned out as a stargazer and I felt as if I were dying.

"Ramapriya, when you first came to me you were full of compassion for the suffering alcoholic, were you not?"

"Yes."

"You told me then that you had to share with others what had been given to you, did you not?"

"That is true, Swami."

"When you had been sober for a few years, you wanted to move to Hawaii with a rich lady. She wanted a companion, and you wanted to oblige. I said God wanted you to continue your work; the sun could wait."

He ordered Darjeeling tea and handed me prasad, food consecrated on the altar in the temple.

"A year later you came to counsel with me and you told me you hated Sedona. You said people there were spiritually shallow. You wanted to move to the monastery in Montecito. I said that if you didn't like Sedona, you wouldn't like Montecito. You stayed in Sedona."

Swami is an old man with the razor-sharp memory of a much younger man.

"In India," Swami said, "There is a Sufi story about creation and where to put God. 'If we put God at the bottom of the ocean, man will dive there. Place God on the mountaintop, man will climb there. But if we put God inside him, man will never think to look there.'"

Sometimes I have trouble knowing when natural law is operating in my life. Swami was leading me where I didn't want to go. I always resist, and then the God I cannot see takes over and my life gets better.

"Ramapriya, permit the clients to come to you for

counsel, especially when they seem attached to illusion. See God in each one of them long enough, and one day God will reach out and touch you."

"But Swami, there must be more to my life than one-hour sessions with curiosity seekers who think I can magically make their lives better."

As is his character, Swami sat silently with his eyes closed for several minutes. I always suspected that he drifted into samadhi, a deathlike meditative sleep.

"Go home and light a fire under people. Help students find out who they are. Tell them that God remembers what they forgot," Swami said.

He and I had a silent luncheon alone. After we ate we went to the temple and he chanted while I remained quiet. Swami walked me to my car, and as I started the engine, he tapped on my window.

"Ramapriya, you said to me today that you thought you were dying. You are dying. You are dying for the un-you to become authentic. Stop trying to control everything. God will lead the way. When He is ready for your life to change, your path will bend and you will go there. Your life is not your concern. Fear not. God is building your road as we speak."

In my crisis of wanting more, in looking for the road Swami said God was building for me, I experienced a series of stages, and I want to share that journey with you. Before we can look ahead, we all must look back.

I believe that the root cause of all emotional pain is the divided and un-individuated self. As medical records are carried in the bloodline, so too are all past actions for which we must atone. Alcoholics, drug addicts, and compulsive souls of all sorts oftentimes must die for their disease. Each of us knew the requirements of atoning for past behaviors when we chose to be reborn.

Life on the planet Earth is a reform school. We come back to "take the courses," "learn our lessons," and make evolutionary soul growth. We come back life after life to make amends for the harm we have done to ourselves and others. From the day we are born our ego lies, cajoles, defends, misrepresents, as well as coerces each of us to go to any lengths to get what it, the ego, tells us we must have. We lie and gossip, drug, drink, have illicit sexual affairs, and are dishonest about many other things in our lives. The egocentric world is one of the euphemisms like Devil, Satan, Lucifer, Dark Side, Evil, Mephistopheles, and Beelzebub that describes the split we endure when we turn from the Divine or God within.

What we do unto others we must have done to us. Every single destructive thought or hurtful deed we have done to another we must feel by having the same thing happen to us. When we surrender to the power of the Divine or God within we begin to return to the Creator and in order to do so, we must make amends to free us of our devious past.

We reincarnate not only to refine the soul but to understand Natural Law—that we are all the same: a precious child of God and a divine spirit having a human experience. Each of us has a mission, but because we live in a culture that worships fame and wealth, we diminish those who appear ordinary. Interrelated and interconnected are our watchwords for seeing the world as One—each with his own lessons to learn, and stages on which to play—but all of us are on assignment to come back to the Creator as redeemed fallen angels and errant prodigals—now self-realized as One with the Divine and with one another.

Through years of studying Eastern religions and paranormal psychology, I learned to trust my gut instinct. I have felt and believed there is a God part of me—my High Self. I am neither special nor privileged. Every person has his own High Self guide who can help him detach from what others believe or say.

Each of us is divided into three selves: a low self, a middle self, and a High Self. The low self is ego, which is pleasure bound. The middle self is mediator, which is truth bound. The High Self is God, who is the Great Redeemer.

To find your High Self, you must be clear to hear the voice of inspiration—the God part of you. To be clear means to rid yourself of the chaos that stifles the still, small voice of intuition.

My High Self—the God within me—revealed Himself* to me, reaching out and touching me, as Swami said He would.

*I have used the masculine pronouns, both for people and God/Divine for convenience, and not in a gender-dependent way.

CHAPTER 1

Reconnecting to the Light

There is a part of every person that is divine. In the bustle of our everyday lives, struggling with work, trying to create meaningful relationships with friends and family, we neglect the divine in us. We become distracted by temptations such as alcohol and drugs, obsessions with food or sex, and we misplace emphasis on what seems to be important. The buzz of the world around us can override the divine within.

There are times when the divine sneaks out into the open. Perhaps you've heard a little voice in your head advising you about what steps to take in your life. Or you've heard your "conscience" talking when you're debating the best action. Or when you reflect silently, alone, you feel a presence of someone, something, speaking out at you.

These are the moments when your High Self is trying to make an appearance through your overwhelmed thoughts.

As I said in the prologue, each of us is divided into three selves. The low self is ego—the part of our self that mediates between the world and our natural human appetites for food, love, self-esteem, sexual gratification, intellectual stimulation, and companionship. Problems for many of us arise because the ego, while on a worthy mission, has no sense of proportion. It has a tendency to say things like, "You want a cookie? How about a whole box? Why stop at one glass of wine when you can drink every drop you can get your hands on?" Unleavened by our higher nature, ego lacks the moral and spiritual forces that add balance and proportion to our lives. Ego on its own will not acknowledge itself as part of the larger whole, which demands fairness, sharing, balance, harmony, and community. The ego can help you flourish in the world, but if you let it take hold of you, it can also sabotage.

The middle self is the open-minded, more reasonable side of us. It is the one capable of redemption from egocentric behavior through reeducation. The middle self is the bridge from darkness into light, from receiving for the self alone to receiving the light to share.

The High Self is God.

It's not the God of ancient tales where the clouds part and a bright bolt of lightning descends from the heavens. It's not a spirit or an entity that comes down and takes over your body and mind.

There are channelers who purport to communicate with entities. Simply put, an entity is a dead person who won't go where dead people are supposed to go. They hang around and oftentimes become troublesome for those of us still alive. J. Z. Knight, a medium who recently appeared in the film *What the Bleep Do We Know?*, claims that a five-million-year-old being whom she calls Ramtha speaks through her. Your High Self is not such a being. I am uncertain about channeling. Something about invoking spirit contact doesn't click with me. However, some people seem to be helped by it. I suggest you approach such communication with healthy skepticism.

But just because I think channelers are a questionable lot doesn't mean this stuff is not coming from somewhere.

The High Self is something simpler. God is, and always has been, inside of you. You simply haven't been able or ready to meet Him. In meditation, when your mind is still and the will is receptive, you can find your High Self. I found mine then, or, I should probably say, my High Self found me.

ENCOUNTERING MY HIGH SELF

One day, I slipped my favorite CD into the entertainment console as I lay on my bed to reflect on the day's activities. And then, as if guided by a breath coach, I began to breathe as I do when I am meditating: a repetition of deep, slow breaths, in through the nose and out through the mouth. Soon my inhales and exhales became deeper and more rhythmic. My body felt weightless.

Oddly, within a few minutes my lips began to tingle and I struggled to catch my breath. I had the impression that someone was trying to speak through me. I have never been a believer in channelers, so fear caused me to wake up, which silenced whoever wanted to speak. I closed my eyes again and took several relaxing breaths. I let go completely and spiraled into darkness where there were intermittent flashes of bright light.

I focused on a white pyramid. Images of pyramids had first appeared in my daydreams when I was a boy. Now, a powerful and resonant male voice spoke.

Albert, why did it take you so long to talk with me?

"Oh, my God, who is this?" I lashed out.

I was startled awake and sat on the edge of the bed. Where was this voice coming from? I paced the room, swallowing large gulps of mineral water. For years I had heard that some of my friends communicated with dead people. I wanted nothing to do with an entity from the spirit world. Was that what this man was?

However, energy pulled me back to the bed. I lay down and slipped back into meditation.

Relax. Continue to breathe evenly and you will gradually let go of fear. I have been monitoring you. Your actions and thoughts indicate that you are ready to communicate with me mind to mind.

The clearest explanation I can give of this energy connection is that the communication was intuitive. I did not and still do not have out-loud conversations with this invisible guide. The odd thing is that instinctively I had always known there was a part of me that had never exposed itself. Although I would over time ask a million questions to validate him, I somehow instantly knew that this being has kept me alive and sane throughout my life. Through the years I have counseled a lot of clients who swear they have connected with someone "inside" who they could not talk about for fear of being labeled crazy.

I was not afraid, but I wanted proof of who had me under his spell. I instinctively knew he was scanning my intelligence. These thought impressions came to me with ease and authority.

I have been trying to talk to you for more than ten years.

"Why?" I asked.

You teach students that God is within. I am here to remind you that you're someone other than who you think you are. I am the microcosmic God. I am Paul, your High Self guide and teacher. When you reach the deepest level of consciousness I am that part of you who speaks. I am here to help you see things more clearly, as well as to confirm what you know and what more you have to remember.

If truth be told, all my life, at some level, I had been anticipating a connection—a validation of everything I knew to be true for me. To be able to exchange ideas with and ask questions of a source like Paul made lifelong struggles with my identity worth every minute of the pain of separation and alienation from everybody in my life. To know that Paul was me and I was him satisfied my need not to give my power away and not to be controlled by any person or group, particularly by church dogma.

"A few minutes ago while I was in meditation I felt you were forcing yourself on me. I don't want anyone invading me against my free will," I said.

Because you were at such a deep level of consciousness, it seemed as if I were trying to talk through you. I am a part of you and will communicate only to you. You will decide what information you share with others.

"Are you an alien? Have you come to abduct me?" I asked.

Albert, I am not foreign to you and I have not come to take you away. I am the all-seeing, all-knowing part of you connected to the continuum of time. You and I are like spiritual twins.

Aha! Both in humor and in dead seriousness I have said that there were two Alberts. As Paul spoke to me, I did a gut check to see if I agreed with him. On all accounts, what he said rang true.

"Do you intend to dominate me with mind control?"

No. You have a mind of your own, which is controlled by what people think of you and what you must do to be accepted by others. You need to learn to be your own authority.

Paul explained that each person has his own High Self guide, but many people aren't prepared to hear Him or Her. When I asked Paul why he only spoke to me in meditation, he said that during my everyday life, I am too scattered to listen to guidance. But in meditation, when my mind is clear, I can more easily be counseled without conscious contact with him. He and I would be as one.

I would speak as Albert, but the source of the information would be Paul, my High Self. All of this rang true to me, even though I often felt my mind furtive and restless. Paul suggested I should change my ways if I wanted to be able to let my High Self guide me.

One question addressed a trust issue. "If you are an aspect of me and not a separate entity, why do you call yourself Paul?"

Assigning a name distinguishes who is speaking. You need to know whether it is your ego influencing you or your High Self that is talking. Until now you were never able to get out from under the influence of your ego long enough to hear me.

Anyone who wants to contact his High Self can. Advise students to sit quietly each day at a set time and call a name intuitively, as you did with me. Making an appointment at the same time each day increases the possibility of contact with one's soul whisperer.

Today you were afraid of me because I called your name. You never trusted that I would be able to communicate with you. You have lived in fear and distrust. I broke through the defense lines of your ego. Before, I intuitively influenced you without your conscious awareness.

Paul said that he is the God within me. He confirmed his presence throughout my life by recalling crises I had endured. When I was six years old, I fell twenty feet onto a gravel yard. My face was cut and scraped and I was unconscious for several minutes, but I had no broken bones.

I took that fall with you. And—remember the car wreck in 1962?

Driving home to Alabama from Charleston Air Force Base with the top down on my brand new white MGB convertible, I fell asleep at the wheel and woke up just in time to swerve right into a ravine. The car hit nose-first, and I was thrown free into deep layers of freshly mown hay. I suffered a mild concussion, but again, no broken bones.

I nudged you before you hit the sixteen-wheeler head-on, guiding you to turn right onto a soft landing.

"How were you able to save my life when others die prematurely?" I asked.

Karma. It was not your time to die. Each person chooses when to be born and when to die.

The soul knows there is no death. The true self knows that the perfect place, the Upper World, is real. Life on Earth is an illusion. The regret one feels when he dies is that he never knew his authentic self and he did not understand the mysteries of life that are all around him.

Death is like going from one room to another. The hell that scared you as a boy is hell on Earth and not a dark, fiery place of condemnation for your sins or your disbelief in Jesus.

The Upper World is perfect-world consciousness, and the Lower World is chaotic. One needs to crack codes of unsolved mysteries to discover his authentic self, so as not to become attached to earthbound illusion.

The reason ancient schools of spiritual teachings used puzzles and riddles and had various levels of initiation was to ensure that only students who were able to transcend ego control were permitted into the schools. These were prerequisites to study and develop spiritually. The ego uses pleasures to entrap. God uses the spirit of the soul to free.

"How will I solve mysteries?" I asked.

Follow your stars.

Paul was confirming what I have been teaching for a long time. Everything you need to know and everywhere you need to go is in your birth chart.

"Paul, why don't I do what I am supposed to do?"

You are attached to material illusion and false perceptions. When you still your mind, you and I can communicate about who you are and what you need to do.

When you were drinking I urged you to take the tougher road back to God. Alcoholism allowed you to tear apart a life that was not working for you. The steps you were to take once sober would lead you to the real person you were born to be. The ego suggested you switch from hard liquor to wine, or that you needed a vacation. The ego never mentioned the name of God. God and forgiveness are anathema to the ego.

I was transfixed as Paul went on to describe the origin of Earth and mankind. Lucifer engaged in a power struggle with God. Angel souls left God and the Upper World—and thus the Lower World, although controlled by the ego, was established as a school for remembering life's lessons, prerequisites for return to the Upper World. (I would come to call these two worlds "here" and "there.") Every deed and thought in contradiction to spiritual laws of the Upper World must be atoned for here on Earth. That part of me, spellbound by the ego, must free itself of the ego's false promises. I cannot access that knowledge of truth, love, beauty, and light as

Albert, but I can as my High Self. When I meditate I can connect to the one-true-God-created soul I always was.

Every soul has a resonance with God. The divine frequency is reactivated initially by remembering what harmony and peace feel like. But the magnetism of the ego is strong; man is drawn back to the pleasure chest. Still, God is alive within every soul.

Paul also told me:

All of you on Earth work off karma from past lives by being in service to others. When a life ends, to have loved and to have served are the only attributes that matter.

The cosmic geometry aligns to support all who seek to go back to God. Watch the heavens and celestial movement. When Venus crosses the Sun in 2012, time as you know it will draw to a close. Configurations and signs of providential change are written in the sky maps.

When these planetary configurations happen, you must have made a choice to clear away blocks and barriers to your true identity, as you have satisfied conditions of karma from the seventy past lives that created it. All human beings live life after life after life.

I did not question Paul further about past lives. I knew intuitively that we have lived thousands of lives, in different galaxies and dimensions.

ENDINGS AND NEW BEGINNINGS

So I have a job to do. I needed to know more about my role on Earth. My High Self said I have satisfied the karmic conditions for this life, but each life has different issues that need to be worked on. For instance, someone who has been unfaithful to a spouse must be reborn to feel what it's like to be betrayed in marriage. That same person may have been charitable, loving and kind, studied to become educated, endured poverty with grace. He may have risen to great heights because past lives had put him or her on the path to become revered and respected, in charge in other areas of his life. Also, we must reincarnate to a subsequent life to correct our past misdoings because we create new karma from lifetime to lifetime as well as work off karma from past lives.

As karma is *a priori,* the still small voice of intuition will dialogue with each of us if we are aware and alert to karmic conditions. That voice will let us know when we are done with reform school on Earth. The cycles of rebirth do end. However, this place, here on Earth, is not reality—this is the illusion that reality created for us to come back to refine the soul and to embrace forever who we really are. And to refine my soul, I needed to understand my purpose.

"What exactly is the assignment?" I asked Paul.

Your assignment is to break away from the ego's control

by clearing past-life and present karma; to make amends for harm that you have done to others; to live better than you speak; and to live justly, love mercy, and walk humbly with God. Past deeds have separated you from God and made you a slave to your ego. You have agreed to clear others with the lessons you find along your path. You have hidden your true identity to protect yourself. You're not who you think you are. And nothing is what it seems. You are of the light.

"Am I the only one to lead others to the light?"

No, Albert, you are not. Liken this to a roundup of souls who want to return home. I have made contact with you as others are becoming reconnected to their High Selves. You were eventually able to hear my contact and to respond. Others will hear their own guidance.

"What is the message?" I queried.

The end of the world of illusion is at hand. The world as it truly is will be made manifest. You must uncover your true self and help others to find their true selves. You are inter-related and interconnected. You will know one another by sound and by light.

I was riveted. Stone-still, I listened, and my heart raced.

There will be a homecoming of prodigals. Souls will come back spiritually balanced, having spent lifetimes looking for the other part of themselves in someone else.

For those who choose to clear, chaos will end. The conflicts that rage within will cease. Millions of souls are beginning to

anticipate this event. The Lower World will be as the Upper World. It is said, "as above, so below."

"It is the end of the world," I whispered through parched lips.

No, it is the beginning of time. Ancient prophecies will give you a deeper understanding of the period of endings and new beginnings.

• • •

I don't believe in Armageddon. The world will not go up in smoke because of man's sins. But what was this coming spiritual revolution all about? Could it be that war in the Middle East will escalate beyond human comprehension? Would there be some divine intervention to end the war? Did this have to do with global warming? My mind was jabbering like a gaggle of geese. A countdown had begun, and I wanted to run.

Computer technology may be the Antichrist, because it sucks so many of us into pornography, gambling, and online trading. Young people obsess over chat rooms and online video games which feed their dark side. On the other hand, cyberspace is the fastest way to get information.

I turned on my laptop and searched for anything I could find about what lies ahead of us. If my intuition could conjure this stuff up, there had to be confirmation or negation somewhere.

I turned my inquiry to the Mayan calendar and the year 2012. Not your run-of-the-mill calendar, the Tzolkin,

as the Mayan calendar is called, originated in at least the sixth century BCE. It is reputed to be the most accurate date book in the world, due in part to its relative complexity; it uses cycles of 13 and 20, relating to the movement of Venus and other planets, and it incorporates twenty-two different subcalendars.

The Mayans approached prophecy by careful study of the periodicity of cycles, especially astronomical ones, and their connection to human events. For the layperson, astrology is an interpretation of what it means when planets are in certain configurations, forming geometric alignments with one another, and especially at critical times such as solar and lunar eclipses and at the equinoxes. We astrologers call astrology the art of interpreting astronomy.

Highlighting the significance of the year 2012 are thirty-two solar and lunar eclipses, looming large between September 2006 and November 28, 2012, and the transit of Pluto through the sign of Capricorn. Pluto transiting through Capricorn means that there will be a mass reconstruction in all areas of government, business, industry, and money markets. The complexion of changes will be conservative rather than radical.

A solar eclipse occurs when the Moon passes in front of the Sun, partially or completely blocking its light. During a lunar eclipse the Earth passes directly in front of the Moon, casting its shadow on the Moon's surface. Eclipses are always powerful benchmarks of change, and most of the time they disrupt and displace people from their familiar and ordinary flow of life. Did you ever read the biblical passage "it rains on the just and the unjust"? We are all affected by celestial phenomena, positively and negatively.

Some astrologers believe that eclipses have less effect on individuals than on aggregate entities—cities and countries, for example, or Wall Street, or Christianity, Islam, or other religions. I disagree. I also disagree with those who track the stars and focus on the negative influences rather than the benefits from everything that happens to us. I have always said that there are no good or bad birth signs; it's what you do with the hand life deals you. When given challenges, do you fold your tent or try harder? Do you embrace change or fight modification to the death? Under lunar eclipses, people often experience in their personal lives a sudden end to one pattern and the beginning of a new cycle. For example, they may change jobs, move to a new town, get married or divorced, or experience financial losses or gains. Financial markets that have been stagnant or negative might see a more positive economic trend. Movies that favored one genre, like action adventure, may give way to films with a more serious message. The same shift may occur for music and books. One of the major transitions that I see looming is a shift in mass consciousness from a religious to a spiritual orientation, especially when Pluto goes into Capricorn on

November 28, 2008, and stays in the sign until March 23, 2023. Eclipses compound change over time, collectively, rather than stark and sudden changes.

Just as lunar eclipses are about endings, solar eclipses indicate beginnings. Three successive solar eclipses set the stage for World War I, and two intense solar eclipses preceded World War II. Just as an architect drafts precise drawings in designing a new building, eclipses are calibrated cosmically—divine designs activate planetary configurations in relation to one another to set the stage for an event. In these instances, they were omens of war. The Korean conflict and the fighting in Vietnam started when the planet Mars was in the sign it ruled, Aries, exacerbated by solar eclipses.

The Mayans were gifted astrologers and astronomers who used the movement of the planets to predict the future. They possessed the knowledge to use what the movement of the stars was telling them—which they have been able to do for centuries—to come to the conclusion that on December 21, 2012, the Mayan calendar will end. Dr. Carl Johan Calleman, author of *The Mayan Calendar* (Garev, 2001) and *The Mayan Calendar and the Transformation of Consciousness* (Bear and Co., 2004), writes that by his calculations the end of the Mayan calendar is to be October 28, 2011.

It is not my purpose to educate you about the Mayan calendar or to debate dates, but rather to let you know what I believe will happen and why. What's a year, give or take? You will soon find out that it's never a specific date but all the things we do or don't do that will lead us to enlightenment or keep us in darkness.

Many prophets, purported authorities, and historians steeped in Mayan culture are writing books about the end of the Mayan calendar. If the information is discernible at all—and most of it reads like gobbledygook—the conclusions appear to question rather than answer what is going to happen to the earth. Fundamentalist Christians are once again using this benchmark to predict the end of the world. Many of these self-proclaimed prophets see a future of wars and rumors of wars, natural disasters, devolving moral compasses, or collapse of global financial markets. I disagree. What happens in the world is contingent more on how we change ourselves to help change the universe for the better.

Haven't we had a turbulent world since Adam bit the apple? There have always been calamities. Many victims of hurricane Katrina have already had their apocalypse, in a sweltering stadium with no privacy and not enough food, water, or toilets. Rescued from rooftops and flotsam-infested water that did not recede for weeks, they may have wished they were dead. Earthquakes have killed hundreds of thousands of people. Floods have destroyed whole cities and villages. Tornadoes have wiped out towns and killed hundreds.

Have we not had wars and rumors of war since the caveman crafted a club? The worst catastrophes have been wars waged in the name of God, when the real reason one country invades another is to control its resources, like gold or oil, or to impose its will on others, depriving them of freedom. True, there are occasional quiet periods when the warlords take a break, but in general man always seems to be fighting somebody over something, usually in the name of God.

You can talk about peace as much as you want. You can go to spiritual conclaves and conferences and listen to countless powder-puff hocus-pocus speeches, but unless each of us changes the way we live and the way we think—including admitting that our God is not the only God—we *will* go up in smoke; the world *will* end with a whimper or, more likely, a bang. If warring nations do not change how they view their God and their tenets and their prophecies, and allow everyone to worship God as he sees fit, we are toast. The movie ends.

We have power over what the Mayan calendar predicts.

The world, made worse by each of us over time, is not headed for death, destruction, and global genocide, unless we fail to change our intent. And although 2012 is a timeline when we will reap what we have sown, the turn-around time is now—not 2011 or 2012. As with the Harmonic Convergence in 1987—a planetary alignment that emphasized the feminine influence in mankind—when changes happened gradually over the next two decades; no colossal event will take place on a specific date; we should open our eyes to what we don't do leading up to the ground-zero dateline. Look at the landscape in your own neighborhood and in the world at large. We don't need Nostradamus to prophesy our fate; our destruction or salvation is in our own hands.

There is time to change, and we must do so. We must feed the poor and share water and other geophysical assets to ensure that our brothers and sisters are taken care of. To avert dire consequences, we just need to transform ourselves. Change yourself to change the world.

My research has reconfirmed the idea that answers and questions are found in the same place—within each of us. Astrology has always been about timing. Swami had said that when it was time for my life to change, the road would bend and I would follow it. The road is bending for all of us.

• • •

I turned off my computer. I wanted some confirmation about my research. I was satisfied that I was in control of my life and that no negative force or source could influence me without my say-so. After four or five minutes of silence, using my breathing exercise, Paul spoke.

I am going to help you remember what you have always known, but illusion has caused you to forget.

"Do you have any suggestions about how to prepare for the end of the Mayan calendar in 2012?"

Discover who you are. Revelations will appear as you need to know them. Do what you are doing. Stay the course. Whatever you do, do not get stuck trying to figure out what the end of the Mayan calendar means—let it be revealed when the time is right. Do not expend your energy contemplating the destruction that may lie ahead. If you don't like weeds, pull them out by their roots. If you like flowers, water and feed them. If you want peace, make peace.

Look within your own akashic record for your answer, Albert. You have lived many depraved lives, yet today you help others. The cosmic system of karmic retribution joins natural law to offer you redemption. You are on the right path now, but you have lived a life as a ruthless soldier in France, another as a demagogue in Russia, yet another as a corrupt barrister in England, and many others, both positive and negative. When you can look honestly at yourself, you will be able to remember all these lives. You must remember in order to make amends and to change. All memory of past lives is within you.

Albert, welcome to the school of remembering. Knowing is born within you. You never learn anything, you remember.

Telepathy signaled you to look for information from teachers and authorities regarding the year 2012. Your intuition did the rest.

When I need to remember something, the sourcebook

appears right in front of me, or it pops up on an Internet search.

"Paul, all of this seems like a rainbow of miracles. It is as if the Divine has intervened in my life, giving me a new way to live and love and comprehend who I am."

The beauty of miracles, Albert, is that you have been able to transcend the limitations of your Earth dimension. The beauty of miracles is the awakening—the remembrance of things as they truly are meant to be—the breaking with illusion. You are beginning the journey of the discovery of your true self. Miracles are for everyone who can see them and feel them as you have. Mankind is receiving what has been in storage for millennia.

Having looked at separation and emptiness, people must decide to make amends for their behavior. All who want to reconnect to their authentic selves will be able to activate a homing effect, the pitch and octave of which will allow them to recognize themselves as precious children of God.

You are intrigued with mystery and buried treasure. You seek to discover the hall of records and to uncover the Holy Grail. Better you should ask the question, "Who am I?"

To begin the return home, know that the hall of records—where you have been and where you need to return—is buried within you, not under the sphinx or on a remote mountaintop. The hall of records is where God is, within man.

"You have talked about being equally yoked—not getting on the path with those whose intentions are less aligned with spirit than mine. Are we attracted or repelled by the sound of someone's voice?" I asked.

Yes. This phenomenon is called imprinting. Hear a man's voice and you will like him immediately or want to flee his presence. You will have an inner confirmation as to whether the person in question is in alignment with your own soul matrix.

All world leaders have the power of resonance. Many use their voices with positive results. Actors, teachers, politicians, industrialists, and ministers sway people. Adolf Hitler, Benito Mussolini, Josef Stalin, and many others were calibrated with the message of darkness.

You must admit how egocentric concepts, self-centered ideas, hurtful deeds, harsh words, and parasitic mind perversions have kept you in darkness, separated from God, behaving contrary to your true self. Imperative for return to the rekindled light within is purification. A cleansing—which requires dispensing with false disguises and bogus identification—will reveal who you truly are: a precious child of God.

To clear means to repudiate thoughts and deeds committed by adhering to persuasions of the ego, this cannot be accomplished with occasional meditation and sporadic prayer or spiritual revival or momentary relief through song or seminar. Man is sick at a deep soul level.

In these times leading up to 2012, an interdimensional door will open. There will be a consciousness jolt and shift. Man will wake up to God-self and want to go home—bal-

anced. But the price is to clear what has caused the separa-tion from the Creator.

One final answer to your question of what you are trying to clear: As a surgeon probes a patient to remove every cell of cancer, or a composer fine-tunes his concerto to eliminate every false note, mankind must clean up the karmic misdeeds that stand between us and God. It is time to return home.

Slowly I awakened on my bed, much like a deep-sea diver surfacing. I stretched and yawned and hopped out of bed. In order to capture what I had experienced, I recorded in my journal all the insights Paul had just imparted.

Questions danced in my head. Why had I felt all my life that I had little connection to my family? Why did I choose alcoholism as a means to get back to God? How can we be someone other than who we are? Have I been living in a drama that made me face karma—my past misdeeds—before I could get to my true purpose in life?

The answers were apparently to be found within myself by means of intuition. The reason I could not know the answer to the question "Who am I?" was that my ego had camouflaged my true identity with lies. I was ready to find true purpose for my life. The following chapters detail the stages that I experienced on my own spiritual journey. I now offer them here with the hope that they will help to guide you on yours.

CHAPTER 2

Stage One—Converting the Ego

In my own understanding of the word, the ego was how I interacted with the world to satisfy my own desires. Sometimes my ego served me well. It helped me make my way in the world in a fair and conscientious manner. But for most of my adult life my ego had gotten way out of control. And when that happened I had gotten into trouble, big trouble.

Allowing ego to run your life will distract you from that which is truly meaningful. In unlikely moments it can subvert and corrupt your best intentions with webs of deceit and disingenuousness. Just when you are about to connect the paradigm dots to reveal a soul mystery—to see more clearly the dark part of you and how it can be enlightened—the ego becomes specious and deflects your attention with doubt and distrust.

Going underground—oozing into the lower layers of your subconscious—the ego will undermine your capacity to reason and to escape its malfeasance. This is your opportunity to hear the whisper of your inner voice trying to illumine the game plan of the ego. Ego, mischievous and diabolical, wants you to believe that it is the freer and more fun part of you. Be on your guard. The ego can start out playful, then become treacherous and ultimately put you in harm's way.

Ego isn't a dirty word. Ego isn't the enemy. Yet it must be converted and it must be retrained. The ego can become a positive and powerful force to get us all back to God. Ego rules the world of illusion, and at times it tries to trick us into believing that its chicanery is real and the spiritual path is nonsense. Ego receives for the self alone.

I have always been a fan of Joseph Campbell, a transpersonal psychologist and author, whose thinking was heavily influenced by the theories of Freud and Jung. Campbell touched on the subject of ego in his mythological version of Earth's creation. In *The Power of Myth*, Campbell describes the rebellion of Lucifer and his minions, how they left paradise and set up camp on Earth, which God had set aside for these outcasts. To stay in the

Order of Lucifer, fallen angels took a vow never to say the name of God. Campbell contended that all of us are fallen angels, separated from God by lawless egos, and that our redemption can come only when we speak to God directly and learn to make better choices.

Looking back at my own life, I had to admit that despite all of my conventional religious training I never really felt connected to God. Quite the opposite. From the time I was a little boy, I often felt lonely and afraid. Much like a ventriloquist's dummy, I had been doing what my ego drove me to do out of some misguided idea that this would bring peace and control. In the absence of true spirituality, my ego had taken charge of me, helping to create a life of illusion and deception woven around addictions. The authentic me, the child of God, had been pushed to the background. I remember that I felt like one groping in the dark to find a safe place—a place where what I sensed did exist, but it seemed I was searching alone.

This was an interesting paradox to me. I understood I needed to rein my ego in, but how? And then it dawned on me: like two kids whose ankles are tied together in a three-legged race, my ego and I must cooperate, work together to find a balance. I remembered a verse I had learned as a boy at church, "Out of the depths I cry to thee, Lord hear my prayer, let thine ears be attended to the voice of thy supplicant." I would cry out and then I would listen. And what I would hear would guide me.

Swami once told me if you love the ego, you can convert it to serve as a doorkeeper to higher consciousness. And the wise man was correct. Remembering the true character of my ego has heightened my awareness of how the ego lies to me.

The idea that the ego is a sinister part of us has been reinforced by many religions, which make self-annihilation the goal of spiritual growth. The path of self-annihilation may work for those who intend to live their lives sheltered from everyday realities, in the confines of ashrams or monasteries, but for the rest of us, nothing could be more impractical. We are trying to make our way in the material world and still be spiritual beings.

BALANCING THE MATERIAL AND THE SPIRITUAL

How can we accomplish this balancing to which we aspire? Who among us has the blueprint to balance material comfort "here" on Earth with spiritual sustenance emanating from "there"? How are we to balance healthy relationships with friends and family without subverting a relationship with our High Self? What can we do to balance the temptation to drink and smoke and eat as our egos wish with our need to reach into our depths to find that which will truly satisfy our souls?

Just as the ego, your lower self, has its own heinous modus operandi when unchecked or unchallenged, your middle self, the open-minded part of you, is able to attract people, circumstances, books, concepts, and principles that stir the soul awake. In the natural progression of your day or week or month or year, you will have rescues from the grasp of your ego. A song like *Count Your Blessings Instead of Sheep* can snap you back into gratitude from bramble bushes of lack. Or a book like *The Secret* arrives in your hands to teach you that you get what you deserve in life—you're not a victim. These apparent random coincidences are able to help you escape the clutches of the ego and find a firmer footing.

The goal is an ego that co-exists with a healthy conscience. The first techniques I suggest to bring your ego into balance are visualization and dialogue. They will help to reach a part of you that has been hidden from you for much of your life. While you have been out in the open and held accountable for your actions, your ego has been in hiding. Although your ego has been at the bottom of the things you've done, it has not been held accountable, because it has been silent and invisible.

I encourage clients to conceptualize the ego not only as shadow but also as a twin self. The thoughts and actions of both you and your ego create all of your negative and positive qualities.

First close your eyes. See yourself opening your arms as you would to greet a friend. Now, embrace your ego, the mischief maker who has stirred up all the trouble in your life. You may see your ego as all your defects and un-controlled appetites rolled into one. After your embrace, step back and ask your ego to sit down. Just as if he were an actual person, talk with him. Let him know that you are not absolving yourself for your difficulties, and you need him to face your character defects with you.

The talk might go something like this:

You: "We're in a mess, you and I. What's going on?"

Ego: "I didn't get what I wanted. I wanted to do what I wanted to do when I wanted to do it. No controls. No limits. I encouraged you to eat and drink and buy what you wanted, go where you wanted, and not have to pay for a thing. I even showed you how to treat others so they would know who was boss. What's the problem?"

You: "The problem is obvious. Each person needs to live in balance and in sanity, so they can hear God's voice when He speaks. You're not acknowledging how afraid I became because of you, not to mention the hundreds of shameful things we did together. Moving in the middle of the night to avoid creditors or always having to make new friends because we drove the ones we had away."

Ego: "I know you weren't happy with the way things were."

You: "First, we are going to believe it's possible to change.

No situation is hopeless unless we adopt a pessimistic outlook or decide to become a permanent victim. Second, God will help us if we ask Him to. The universe is good and He is our source. We've been hoodwinking ourselves all our lives and now it is time to take our spirit back."

Ego: "What if I don't like living the way you are suggesting?"

You: "God will let you live in misery; he's permissive."

Ego: "Him? How do you know He will want me back?"

You: "Ego, if He's taken me, he'll take you."

Ego: "I'm afraid that just saying His name will kill me."

You: "I'll help you. Let's start by spelling it. Here we go together."

You and Ego: "G-O-D. God."

This dialogue bears the hallmarks of a healthy conversation with the ego. First, it's friendly. We don't get anywhere by beating ourselves up. The process of transformation begins with self-acceptance. Second, it's effective. Some people believe it takes forever to get back into God's graces. However, it is amazing how quickly things begin to turn around when you feel that your ego and you are aligned in purpose. My clients have testified to this. One client recently commented, "I never had a clue that somebody with my checkered past could feel so free once I stopped blaming my ego and cleaned up my act."

Finally, a dialogue between self and ego like this sample is transformative. Once there is a true coming to terms with the ego, many people experience a breakthrough. Coming to honest terms with self is the first step in the spiritual experience, just as the caterpillar must spend time in a cocoon before becoming a butterfly. When you confront your ego, you can have a happier, freer life.

The ego is not our enemy. The ego is our strongest ally. But it must go through a psychic change. There is a powerful transcendence that happens when the ego confesses to how it has misled us.

When I was in college, the teachings of Swiss psychotherapist Carl Jung rang true for me. He used astrology birth charts to diagnose a patient's difficulties. Jung refused to see a patient who would not let him use astrology to guide the therapy.

Jung's father was a minister in the Swiss Reformed Church, and several of his uncles were parsons. Very early in his life, Jung experienced dreams and visions that convinced him that religion was a personal matter that had little to do with established creeds. He also was convinced that God had a "dark" side—which he later determined was man's ego—which did not accord with the conventional Christian image of an ever-loving father. Jung found himself in the position of being unable to subscribe to the faith on which he had been reared, yet at the same time he continued to believe that individuals could be neither happy nor healthy unless they acknowledged their dependence upon some higher power rather than upon the ego.

The strongest argument Jung offered for the realized self was when he explained the collective unconscious, which is a reservoir of the experiences of our species. He said the collective unconscious part of us must awaken, become conscious, and that the ego must redeem the self by being individuated. Individuation can only happen when we turn away from the crowd and find our answers within ourselves—when we cease to care what others think of us and our behavior.

The ego can either be fed or faced. It's like having a tame dog and a mad dog living within you. When you pray and meditate, see God in everyone, and live in truth, the tame dog wins. When you live in darkness, blame others, and refuse to pray and meditate and change, the mad dog prevails. Which one is winning within you? The one you're feeding!

FACING THE EGO'S PAST

What I know without doubt is that I have listened to my ego through many lifetimes with the same destructive results. One particular incident several years ago comes to mind that still causes me great pain.

It was the Christmas of 1978. I had returned to Birmingham to spend the holidays with my family, and my mother Maggie invited me to stay with her. Her apartment was attractive but small. I was a full-blown alcoholic at the time, and I should have stayed in a hotel.

On Christmas Eve I'd been on an all-day ho-ho holiday toot. When I walked through the door, two hours late, my mother glared at me, hands on her hips.

"You ought to be ashamed of yourself, coming into my house drunk as a skunk. Some things never change. If you don't know how to respect me, stay away."

I had been at a college friend's house drinking from lunch until after six o'clock. My mother had been expecting me to take her to a party at my sister's. Couldn't she understand that I was just having a few drinks with a friend and his wife?

The ego struck the match and the fires of fear. I pulled out all the stops and leveled my 110-pound, five-foot-tall mother: "You're nothing but a goddamned bitch. I hate you. You've been a martyr since the day Daddy left you high and dry with six kids. I wish you were dead."

Mother had been dressing; she was putting on her good jewelry, most of which had been gifts from me. Without a word, she turned and walked into her bedroom. She meticulously boxed everything I had ever given her and came back into the living room carrying the tiny boxes.

"Here. Take this. I don't want any of it. I never want anything from you again as long as I live." Then she left the room, slamming the door, leaving me alone in my shame.

And Maggie, whom I'd called the queen of hearts since her open-heart surgery the year before, the mother who had paid off loans and fielded hostile telephone calls from my creditors, who had lain awake nights wondering if I would come alive home from a drunken all-nighter, and my biggest defender behind my back and detractor to my face, cried, and prostrate outside her bedroom door, I heard her heart break.

The little boy who won spelling bees and poetry festivals in grade school, made all A's in high school, and had perfect attendance in Sunday school—a God-fearing, sweet-as-pie Southern gentleman—grew up to cut his mother to ribbons rather than face his own demons. It is the nature of a runaway ego, deadly as a king cobra and no respecter of persons, not even my own mother.

After I got sober in 1980, I made direct amends to my mother for all the lies I'd told, the bad loans she'd co-signed, the killing words I'd spoken, and the blame I'd laid at her feet. And when Maggie lay dying in March 1996, I held her hand, kissed her wrinkled face, wept deep tears of sorrow and gratitude for having her as my mother, and watched her spirit leave her body. My clearing—making amends to those I had harmed and changing my behavior, emotionally, financially, and spiritually—left time to heal what our respective karmas demanded we experience and forgive. We were two distinctly different people, but I came to love and adore her. The same thing happened with my absentee father. The day before he died I made amends with him. Both my parents were great teachers.

Making amends put a great distance between my contrite true self and my unethical and rambunctious ego. How did I know to find my true self through seeking forgiveness? The voice of inspiration guided me with humility to right wrongs. How was this right action a key element in my transformation? I found peace that had eluded me for years and years. I was inspired to ask my ego: "Are you a devil who chases me or an angel who has come to help me?" And in that moment—with that question—something miraculous happened. My ego, the dark side of me, died. My ego, as the phoenix, rose from the ashes, morphing spiritually so that I became a precious child of God. My High Self was able to connect me to the natural law that the ego must be challenged to hold the light of the precious child of God daily. To maintain the ability to think, speak, work, play, and communicate with others as who I was born to be, I must be diligent to keep the ego responsive to the Divine within me.

Are there souls who never make it back home? What happens to them? Many lost souls refuse to reform. They cling to remnants of the ego as a drowning man does to a life raft.

Like runaway children who leave home when they don't want to follow their parents' house rules, these souls reenter Earth's vibration and are drawn through the law of attraction to human beings who have become captive to addictions like alcohol, drugs, and sex and who wallow in anger, rage, and resentments.

I began to understand more clearly how the ego palmed off a life on man that man could not support. Man was never who the ego told him he was, and the day of reckoning would come sooner rather than later. I thought of the emperor's "clothing." We keep supporting something that does not exist.

The unredeemed ego is what keeps us connected to the never-ending karmic cycles. Just as the soul can progress and make giant steps toward redemption and release from the wheels of karma, an uneducated and godless ego—one never challenged and one never able to shift from the darkness into the light of true self—keeps us attached to repetitive lives through devolution rather than evolution.

But there is an awakening approaching. There is an opportunity for the first time in the history of mankind for the least aware and most unresponsive souls to convert the ego. This will be the time of miracles for those who are ready to receive them.

CHAPTER 3

Stage Two—Answering the Question, "God or No God?"

I remember vividly the moment I said "Adios, God." When I was twenty years old I took my first drink. It led to my first experience being drunk and my decision to throw God out. A sassy sixty-something blond gay divorcée in a hotel room in Alabama put that martini in my hands, and I was off and running for twenty years of wild and woolly living—without any sense of right and wrong or care and concern for my actions. It was not, "All of a sudden I broke out into alcoholism." At an unconscious level I had been planning something, anything, to quit being someone I was not. Those two decades of drunkenness could have killed me. Instead, I survived to sort out the difference between my ego and the Divine who wanted to help me live a life worth living. It was my ego who turned me into the Prodigal Son, not God.

DOES GOD EXIST?

Each of us must decide whether there is a God or not. So many of us are more at odds with the liturgies, dogma, "shoulds" and "should nots" of organized religions than we are with the concept of a Power greater than ourselves—but we can't see this distinction when we are in the midst of our frustrations and doubts. Part of the privilege of wrestling with the lack of Divine within our lives implies that our questioning will eventually lead us to an Energy which we can accept as Ultimate Authority. It is the nature of separation from such a Power—the repudiation of a Creator—that stokes the fires of anger and rage at this something or other that we have come to feel is the cause of our difficulties. It is living under the dominion of our ego that is the source of our discontent. The ego is not able to arrange, rearrange, sort through, and make sense of what calamitous misfortunes we meet. But surrender to a Higher Power makes that possible. We must go through many dark nights and oftentimes addictive clouds before we can return to this Master Authority.

It is not possible to convince someone that there is a God. The multi-marketing joy juice, the "come to Jesus" overkill approach of trying to cram God down someone's throat, never works. The reliance upon a Divine which is within us requires self-determination and taking responsibility for our behavior. Many of us are like free-range chickens, plucking and clucking willy-nilly. The God within me does not coddle and coo over the errant Albert. As my mother did when I was acting out, God says to me, "You overspent, now repay. You are fat, now lose it. Drink and you pay the consequences." (Yes, it helps to personalize God and to dialogue with Him or Her—whatever is your perception of the Divine.) More than letting me get by with anything, the God within me loves me no matter what I do, but he will not clean up my messes or excuse my bad behavior. This is the piece that the nonbeliever must embrace. Most of us who throw God out or refuse to accept him have done so because the "I want what I want when I want it" spoiled brat within us eschews the notion of God when our self-centered thoughts and actions meet with resistance.

It is not the God or no-God debate, but rather the wrong use of will of the Ego that persuades us to give up the great and abiding personal relationship with the one who made us, our Creator.

The Roman Catholic Spanish philosopher Unamuno

y Jugo said, "Those who deny God deny Him because of their despair at not finding Him."

If we say, "No God," we have to keep looking. God *is* within each of us as Vedanta teaches. I have come to understand that a macrocosmic God, Brahmin, watches over all of us, and a microcosmic God, Atman, which is within each of us, is energetically connected to the Big God.

MY PAST WITH GOD

As a child, the idea of God drew me in. The prayers, the music, the stories of ancient times, all stimulated my imagination and made me want more. But as I grew older, though I appeared to be a good Baptist, I wasn't satisfied with the God I heard about in church.

What struck a false note was the idea that the Baptist way was the only way. When I read about other cultures and ethnicities with their own tenets and their own God, I questioned if the Baptist faith wasn't more exclusive than inclusive.

I grew up before and during the Civil Rights movement. Churches were segregated. I definitely believed in separation of church and state but I was appalled by the separation of whites and blacks. If there was a God who ordained Baptists to preach that party line, I wanted out of the party.

I was oftentimes unable to feel the presence of God. What I sensed instead was a caste system—there was a hierarchy in our church. The small group that ran the organization were the "leaders" and the rest of us were the followers. There was so much testimony about the spirit of God and how He moved men and women and children and opened their hearts—but it was all a cover-up for what really went on in the church. Chaos and control seemed to be by-laws.

One day I peeked behind the curtain and did not like what I saw. So with the help of too much booze, I skedaddled.

I had too many questions that went unanswered. I dubbed myself president of the debate society. "If there is a God, why is there so much poverty in the world? If God loves us, why does he allow wars to go on and on and on? And why do innocent babies die at birth?"

When I sobered up in 1980 I began to find a power and strength from, and a connection to, the Divine by facing down my bad-boy behavior. It became apparent that it was I, not God, who drank and drugged and bought things I did not pay for. Unlike Geraldine, the character Flip Wilson played in drag, who was wont to say every time she got caught in some cockamamie scheme, "The devil made me do it," I had to fess up that it was just me and my shadow who were at fault.

I had to take a fearless and thorough moral inventory

63

see her one Sunday morning very early and stayed until three o'clock the next morning. It was one of the most interesting days of my life.

I wanted to tap her brain about my past lives. I asked Gina whether or not I had actually been a centurion—a Roman army officer. She replied that if I were very clear and open to past lives, I would be inspired in meditation with honest and objective answers.

Exactly as she predicted I have seen in meditation and in dreams the past life when I was a Roman soldier who broke the feet of Christians being crucified. I have consulted with a couple of seers who have verified this for me as well. It aligned with what Paul says to me, "We must feel every single thing that we have ever done to harm or injure another. We must endure the same suffering."

I have come to know that I had club feet because I broke the feet of convicted criminals around the time of Christ—boomerang karma about how I inflicted pain on others. My intuition seemed to say to me, "You want to know how painful your acts were? Here are the feet to remind you." My club feet were also a reminder to stand on my own two feet.

I have learned why a lot of things happened in former lives and in this one. In this life I took issue with Catholicism. In a former life I had been a Vatican ruler. I made rules and regulations and saw that they were enforced. Today, as penance, I must help clear away the addictions and confusions of my clients—consort with and comfort them, not judge them—and I must do so without prejudice regarding religious beliefs and without a rigid point of view. In many ways this life is to atone for that one in Rome. It is odd, but true, that I feel I learn much more from my clients than they do from me.

But I have had the greatest difficulty in knowing who God is and what He expects of me. I have had the same trouble with God that all mankind has had, because we look for Him in the same way: We try to figure out who God is, instead of allowing Him to reveal Himself.

Here are some things I did to find God: A meditation teacher led me to be quiet and to listen to the God within me. I began the practice of yoga—the spiritual discipline and techniques of meditation that enabled me to achieve knowledge of God. I disciplined myself to quietude every day at a set time. God touched me and opened my heart. My sneaky mind eventually gave way to tranquil contemplation.

The longer you pray and meditate, the more quickly God will speak to you and the sooner you will live with inspiration and courage instead of fear.

I often look everywhere outside myself for solutions. God is within, just as the ego is a part of me. God is the creator of all, including the ego. The role of the God within is to love and guide us when we will allow it.

God is permissive and will allow us to make poor

choices and unwise decisions—to be as errant and mischievous as we want to be. However, we will pay the price by being isolated and separated from God: If we drink too much, we go to jail; couple indiscriminately, get a disease; judge another, we're convicted. God has not wreaked havoc on us. We create our own reality.

God will wait patiently for us to get sick and tired of bad-boy and bad-girl behavior. When we turn everything over to God, our lives will be worth living. Ego tries to divide, separate, and deceive us with self-importance, while God says that we are all His precious children.

HOW I SEE GOD

My interest in the Vedanta Society led to how I view God today. I found in the Vedas the first strong evidence that God loved me and had certain requirements of me. These Hindu scriptures rang true for me—I got a gut check that these teachings were my path and they suggested that God was within me. I had been sober for a few years when I joined Vedanta, so this additional spiritual checkpoint enhanced my relationship with a Power greater than me.

Vedanta relies on its followers to practice meditation. The world is so noisy and there are so many hucksters promoting "isms" and religious beliefs that Vedanta's attitude about how to know God appealed to me.

When I visit the Sarada Convent, an order of the Vedanta Society in Montecito, I am always a bit irreverent with its spiritual residents, who are called nuns. While they meditate I sometimes count the number of squares in the ceiling of the temple or swipe prasad from the altar before it is blessed. I look upon them as my sisters and I am their brother. The Sarada Convent is a safe house for these women to contemplate God and to be of service to devotees. Before initiation, they are on probation for one year, and they take their final vows after ten years. Probation gives the newcomer a chance to see if lifelong service in Vedanta is a fit or if it's time to do something else with her life.

The nuns run a bookstore, where I shop as much for baubles as for books, which cover all religions of the world. Nightly vespers and Sunday services take place in a temple perched amidst oleanders, cymbidia, and ceanothus, as well as olive and oak trees, Monterey pines, and eucalypti.

I met the nuns when a friend asked me to prepare and interpret astrology charts for them. As God-filled as these sweet peas are, life in a convent is not all Hallelujah Chorus. They struggle with God's will and sometimes fight among themselves. When I first met them I assumed they were anchored, locked, and sealed in Godness and goodness—that they never had a bad day and all was loveliness and light. Not true. A few women have left the order because they wanted to return to the world—or because they could no longer put up with the other nuns. Their dilemmas remind me that all of us are human and that no one is safe from the temptations of the ego, especially aspirants who live in a religious order whose purpose is to seek God.

When I was first initiated into Vedanta, I wanted everyone I knew to join. Today I only want those who are drawn to its teaching to become members. Many times the nuns quietly told me to stop proselytizing. In my early days as a devotee I spoke harshly of the wealthy (the convent is in one of the most affluent neighborhoods in the world) who appeared to prefer their fancy clothes and fine cars and Italian palazzos to God. One of the nuns cautioned, "They'll either get it or they won't. It's not your business. It's God's business."

Many people view Him as a punishing God. If we are not good, if we break the Ten Commandments, if we commit adultery, we will suffer. Most churches use fear and intimidation as a way to bring the errant ones back into line with existing church tenets and beliefs.

I see God as a clown who laughs at how seriously we take ourselves. We make plans, He rearranges. Power brokers roll the dice for world dominance, while God gets a kick out of how we think we are in control. I notice this especially in the geopolitical arena.

Of course, we Americans think that we are right, that

God is on our side, but we forget that He is the God of us all. We invade a country in the name of God and truth, love, and beauty and we lose the battle. Remember Vietnam? Do you really think that we are going to win in Iraq? No, but it is not a matter of God. God is not a God of war. It is rather a case of the war within us spilling out onto the fields of genocide.

Every night as I fall asleep, "Now I lay me down to sleep, I pray the Lord my soul to keep . . ." I ask God to bless all of us, especially those who our talking heads and political and governmental bullies have written into the script as our enemies—they are not mine and they are not God's. So the clown laughs and lets man play his silly games. I laugh with God as well. Trust me—on this point I laugh out loud—a lot!

When I was initiated into the Vedanta Society, some of my friends asked why I would join a religion when I believe in nothing—I know what I know by experience. I repeat what got me to join: "All paths that lead to God are right paths."

The *Bhagavad Gita* reminds us that the war is always within. The gist of the *Bhagavad Gita* is that you meet the enemy and it is always you. No one is trying to do or undo you, except you. The Vedas reinforce the perfectly calibrated footpath for me to follow to freedom.

If you want to see who the enemy is, look inside. If you want to know who is out to get you, look in the mirror. If ego and God are within, that's where the war that can be won is being waged.

God is love, and He allows you to live the life you are willing to pay the price to create. God is constant and eternal. Love does not need to defend and deny. It is the divided ego that maneuvers to keep man in confusion.

God or no God? For me, there is no question that God is within me, and without him I would be absolutely nothing. God offers unconditional love.

I posed the question one day to my guru: "Why do I have trouble with unconditional love?"

"If God and ego are the same, and if both live inside of you, let God speak more and let the ego listen," he told me.

CHAPTER 4

Stage Three—Out of the Darkness and Into the Light

The light and love of God never die, but lie dormant within us. Our High Self connection can awaken the light by receiving that light to share, but not for the self alone. It is never too late to return to God. Through this process of clearing—removing "bread of shame" or an undeserved reward—we can reclaim our authentic self.

Stage Three, out of the darkness and into the light, lets me know that each of us is filled with the light of the Creator, no matter how dimly it shines.

A famous Kabbalah tale addresses this stage brilliantly. During the nine months we spend in our mother's womb, an angel holds a candle for us, teaching us the wisdom of the universe. We behold everything, from the beginning of the world to the end of the world. When we are born, the angel gives us a sharp blow on the upper lip and it makes us forget everything we have learned. Yet memory traces remain in our souls. The idea of God resonates with us, and upon these residual memories we build our consciousness.

When I discussed this with Swami, he said, "You have become less Albert and more who God created you to be. How did this happen?"

"I learned who I am by experiencing a lot of pain being who I am not," I told him. "I have wanted what I wanted and not enough what God wanted for me. I can talk about how evil my ego self is, but more often than not I make choices that align me with the deceitfulness of my ego.

"Will I ever find favor in God's eyes?" I asked him.

"Not if you constantly look. It is the same with God as with man. Find satisfaction within yourself. Love yourself and you will be as popular as the French baker at daybreak," Swami said.

DARKNESS AND LIGHT

"In the beginning God created the
Heaven and the Earth. And the Earth
was without form, and void; and

darkness was upon the face of the
deep. And the Spirit of God moved
upon the face of the waters. And God
said, Let there be light: and there was
light."

—Genesis 1:1–3.

Both my dark side and the light that is within me were created by God. When man refused the light, darkness was created, which I refer to as a Disneyland for miscreants. As God and the ego are one and within me, perhaps twin flames, so are light and dark, day and night parts of divine creation.

Carl Jung wrote that God has a dark side. The devil sought to set up a kingdom of his own by trying to convince man that there was no God. In the nineteenth century, the philosopher Nietzsche stated that God was dead. Jung rediscovered God as a guiding principle of unity within the depths of the individual psyche.

Yes, even God shares our darkness.

God in his mercy created darkness so that man could work out those evil parts of himself that keep him alienated from the Creator. God needs for man to go as far as he can go in the dark and do what darkness demands— receive selfishly for himself. Not only is one relegated to his dark side but he also breaks with his interrelated and interconnected nature.

In the absence of light we can feel the cellular pain of being the un-self—a runaway and errant lost child.

God is light and God is love. The low-self ego is by nature dark and incapable of love. Much like a narcissist, the ego is self-absorbed, selfish, self-centered, and it hoardes and clings to what it wants for itself. It creates the chaos in our lives. It brings us darkness. Although it has moments when the light breaks through, like a vampire it returns to the dark in order to survive.

But each of us also has luminosity, though our pilot light may dim and contemplate "fade to black" when we are shrouded in negative thoughts and deeds. The light of God is the divine spark that was in us at birth. That spark is our eternal cord connection to the One Living God. It is who we are at our deepest core, and it is what we have yet to become. It is our promise that all things are possible if we rekindle the light. In moments of clarity transcending viscosity, our faint pilot light blazes brilliantly and alters our psyche.

Why, then, do we not manifest this incredible beingness of light on Earth? Why are we not at peace? And what is darkness?

We are not at peace because cellular memory stirs us to dim the light. We are not as we were created, and we are not living with what binds us to our true essence of unconditional love. We have become addicted to the pleasure chest of our dark side. It is in this dim state that we revel in whatever distracts us from rededication to being authentic and in the light.

Darkness is God's gift to us. Light can only be revealed from darkness. It is God's permissiveness that lets us turn away from his love and live in the kingdom of desire and darkness. As a parent needs for his child to learn from disobedience, God permits us to come out of darkness and into the light, enveloped in His grace.

FINDING THE LIGHT

When I was getting sober, a handsome Navy lieutenant whom I will call Laurence led a lot of twelve-step meetings, and he was so silly that one day I reproached him, "Laurence, alcoholism is a deadly disease, and all you do is act silly from the podium. Stop joking around. Take recovery more seriously."

"Albert," Laurence said, "We drunks have cried over the rotten things we've done long enough—we have lived in the dark night of the soul. When we sobered up we insisted on enjoying life. Lighten up. The next time I see you, make me laugh." He grinned at me and walked away. I was stunned. But eventually I was able to poke fun at myself before anybody else did. When I learned to laugh, I did lighten up, and more of God's light shone through.

Light comes into us through the power of laughter.

God never leaves us. The light never extinguishes. If God is in us and a part of us, redemption will always be possible. As God is, so are we. We are who we are, even though from time to time we act contrary to our true nature.

Kabbalah teaches that man felt that he did not deserve the light of the Creator and that to continue to receive it without merit was creating "bread of shame," which is an undeserved reward. Man believed that in order to receive the light, he had to earn it. And to do so, he had to move from the chaotic limitations of what Kabbalah refers to as "the 1 percent world" and tap into "the 99 percent world"—which can only be accessed through his sixth sense. The 1 percent world is the domain of darkness, with its implied limitations and abundant chaos. The 99 percent world is what is available to us when we move from darkness into light. This ultimately will lead man to infinite possibilities and to receiving the Creator's light to share, not keeping it for himself alone. Man had to look in all the occult hideouts of evil and with a spark of light from the Divine, illumine his blackened soul.

As soon as I walked through the doors into recovery, a carpenter invited me to have coffee after the meeting. When I had laid out all my schemes for beating my drunk-driving charges—how I intended to go to meetings to make myself look good in court—the carpenter said to me, "Albert, it's not the court system that con-

Gautama Buddha's most significant contribution to the spiritual life of humankind was to insist to his disciples, "Be a light unto yourselves." Ultimately, each of us must make our way through the darkness without any companions, maps, or guides.

FACING YOUR DARKNESS AND YOUR LIGHT

The leap from darkness to light happens in a straightforward manner which I will outline for you, the patient and faithful reader.

I am reminded of the philosopher Søren Kierkegaard who wrote about the *blind leap to faith* in his book *The Concept of Anxiety*. Kierkegaard maintains that the transition from one state of being to another, in this case from darkness into light, can take place only by a "leap"— one can never possess both darkness and light. He implies that you must just leap—mindlessly jump—so that the loving arms of God can catch you—break your fall—and set you straight. Another way of expressing this is that it is a return to the Divine, the Creator.

The leap is analogous to a moment of awakening—a stirring that indelibly marks one for a surrender of sorts, a time when you realize that you have been an imposter to yourself. Something stirs in your soul that signals an ending and a resolution to move into a new territory of discovery. There must be a leap of faith and an align-

cerns us. We love you. And we are going to love you until you learn to love yourself." And they all did. Today, I too love the newcomer to recovery.

Light comes into us through love.

UNDERSTANDING DARKNESS

Since my first trip to Egypt in 1983, my light has grown stronger, and I have become aware that the direction of my life is alchemically changing into one of greater purpose. The aim of my first journey back to Egypt was to wipe clean false perceptions about God and to embrace light by illuminating the dark. Converting the ego through love is the first step toward redemption.

My epiphany—my shift from darkness into the light— came in a small spiritual hot spot in Upper Egypt. Dendera is 60 kilometers north of Luxor on the West Bank of the Nile and the site of the temple of Hathor (a goddess high up in the hierarchy of ancient Egyptian mythological power structure), which contains a hieroglyph that has come to be known as the Dendera Light. Egyptian mythology supports the notion that Hathor represents illumination—a "Saul to Paul" instantaneous converter—and a consciousness connector to all who come to her temple. I entered with a dark heart and left in a flood of healing light.

I went to experience the light in the temple of Dendera for my own clearing.

We cannot clear others until we come clean ourselves. I was learning that my ideas of dark and light had been contrary to natural law.

Darkness is an energy that separates us from God and from love. Darkness tells us that our feelings are real, but that God is not. Darkness tells us that only what we see, feel, touch, and smell are real and that everything else is an illusion. The opposite is true. Where light is absent, mind perversions and unnatural desires arise. The voice of darkness fuels negativity that we experience as hopelessness, fear, anger, envy, and mistrust. Darkness is where man goes to experience the cries and demands of his ego. On a deeper psychological level, the dark represents a reflection of man's thoughts and deeds committed in the absence of God. Darkness is godlessness.

Kabbalah suggests that the ultimate objective of spirituality is not to remove humanity's negative traits or even the existence of evil, but to confront and transform the dark forces within ourselves. It is this struggle that ignites the divine within each of us, allowing us to soar. We must be a light unto ourselves.

God understands man's character. Created in his image, man is not God, but God is in man. Darkness is separation from God. Light is a power source of union and harmony and peace. It cannot judge, because it operates without prejudice, manipulation, arrogance, or need to control. Light is. Darkness is not.

Within each of us is the light. No matt how often we flee into darkness, light al we are honest with ourselves about thing into darkness—drunkenness, drugs, inf stealing, coveting, envying—we become e the light."

Man can return to the light at any tin ties, deacons, elders, or character critics from the light, because the light always will be within man. Light is man's birthri

From time to time, prophets and tea Earth to guide the fallen back to God. Th venerated and worshiped. Their light is b magnetism draws the prodigal. Buddha, the Dalai Lama, and many others hold th its essence to draw others to God. Their erate year after year to perpetuate the te mankind.

The light will never fail. It was in the be ways will be within each of us. When we of darkness, the light weakens, but the ele beams on. When the pain of separation is the prodigal can return to the principle of

To be redeemed by light is to become i by allowing it to work within us. When th darkness becomes dissolved in the light c awareness.

ment with the light emanating from the Deity or Creator. Surrender, plainly put, is the first step to turn *on* the light switch and to deny the *off*. This is akin to coming home or returning from whence you started but coming back to a pure self.

The second progression is to practice, like the pianist would her scales or the dancer his steps, to strengthen one's light through meditation. Going into a quiet and reverent place—inside oneself—and finding a sanctuary distant from the dark enticements. The quietude can be a voice-led practice, music only, or a set of prayers or mantra (specified for the student of light) to stay connected to the Divine and His wishes for your regenerated self. This practice is necessary to maintain the light side of your soul urge.

A third repetition that ensures a safe return to your authentic self is to keep a daily journal—tracking thought impressions and actions you take—to enable you to distinguish when your ego is wiggling its way back into your consciousness and daily life. You can rebuff your ego's dismal dictates by reaffirming that you love it and that you will help it make the transition to the light with you. Remember that the ego wakes up earlier than you do, and that every day it must be reacquainted with its new self: a precious child of God.

To make your deal with the Divine and cancel your contract with the Devil or Dark Side, you must write a life history, reconstructing how you fell from grace and took up a life in the dark. It would help to find a trusted counselor who will hear your entreaty (or confession) to set you free from the past.

The last firm step to living in the light is to change associations. In recovery circles we euphemistically refer to this as "changing playgrounds and playmates." Becoming involved with others who share your propensity for what the light side of the soul desires helps you stay connected to who you have always been.

A bonus for following the outline above is to ask at least one person daily, "What can I do for you?" It is in seeking to help others that your own light will grow stronger day by day.

MY JOURNEY OF DARKNESS AND LIGHT

I returned to Egypt in November 1992 to face both my dark side and my light side. Traveling through Upper and Lower Egypt was tough, especially as I didn't make the journey alone but as a tour escort. Bill Clinton was elected President while we were cruising up the Nile.

To those of us who innately feel that we have had past lives in Egypt—the cradle of spiritual renaissance that still profoundly affects people who are compelled to travel there—such trips are more like a homecoming than a typical vacation. In Egypt mysteries await us to be solved through intuition. An innate connection to a past life there oftentimes awakens us to our life's purpose. I have been to Egypt many times since, and like all travelers there I have many stories to tell about how deeply I've been affected by monuments, digs, people, and music.

Going back to Egypt is like returning to the scene of the crime, because so much of the multi-god worship began there: "I love my clothes, I love my jewels, I love my palace, I love my sex life," and on and on and on. Going back to Egypt allows us to change our priorities and see the folly of being consumed with material things. Our spiritual search is to satisfy the longing of the soul. Egypt enhances and enlarges the challenge to return to your true self by coming back to the light.

Twelve travelers joined me for the trip, and I was responsible for getting them out of bed at the crack of dawn, finding clean, healthy food for breakfast, lunch, and dinner, being on time at designated pickup points, and getting in and out of museums and monuments. Feeding them was akin to trying to get ten-year-olds to the table: "Albert, can't we see one more tomb before lunch?"

Between November and May, the weather is cooler, but reflecting sand is deadly hot even when temperatures are moderate. That's why so many tombs are underground, and heat variance of a few degrees makes a difference.

Streets are filled with hordes of drifting sightseers with cameras flung about their necks and at the advice of their tour guides, their passports and Egyptian pounds hidden beneath their clothing, clutching large bottles of mineral water. Throngs of beggars and hawkers thrust their wares at these captive travelers, from fake glass beads and crinkled postcards to plaster busts of pharaohs and souvenir tee shirts.

There is an alignment of frequency and harmonics between Egypt and Sedona. They both have alchemical properties that geologists measure scientifically. These properties affect even the most unaware people emotionally, psychologically, and spiritually. Very few places have this otherworldly resonance and vibration. These properties magnify and intensify one's tendency toward experiencing the spiritual light versus darkness. Legend contends that Sedona has eight or more whirling energy centers called vortexes which are magnetic (masculine), electric (feminine), or electromagnetic (androgynous). Within these energy force fields, many people feel calmness, while others become unnerved. Some hikers report experiencing a physical or emotional healing in these powerful eddies. Others say they have been spiritually transformed.

Egypt has energy fields, or ley lines, that cover thousands of square miles. Ley lines are hypothetical alignments of a number of places of geographical interest, such as pyramids, monuments, and burial grounds. In New Age parlance, ley lines and their intersection points are believed to put out a special psychic or mystical energy. Credence to such phenomena has grown through a new area of archaeological study, archaeogeodesy—the study of the physical properties of the gravity field of the earth—which was practiced in ancient times. Hence, what was once attributed to flights of fantasy or a hyperactive imagination is now gaining greater acceptance as science meets spirituality. There is a theory that memory banks of spiritual wizardry, specifically alchemical secrets—turning base metal into gold or dark energy into transcendent light—as well as clairvoyance and miracle healing, are stored in these energy fields. Many of us believe that we have been in these places in a past life or lives, as teachers and alchemists, and we are returning to stimulate that memory and reactivate those powers.

Hopi elders say that we who come to visit or live in Sedona are ancestors of Egypt. Egypt draws me, just as Sedona lures travelers to meditate and feel her transcendent vortexes. Our travel group gathers along the mystical Nile for reunion.

I was eager to know what I would see and hear in Abu Simbel, the monument to Ramses II; at the Valley of the Kings and Queens, particularly the shrine dedicated to Hatshepsut, the only woman ever to rule Egypt; during the light shows in the temples of Luxor and Karnak; and visiting again the many ancient digs, tombs, museums, and antiquities.

Many people who tour Egypt are looking for the "aha" that so many books about this ancient land promise. There are tour guides who intimate that a traveler just might feel the presence of a spirit, as Napoleon Bonaparte reportedly did when he slept in the Great Pyramid; or receive a profound omen about when the world will end and how; or perhaps channel Cleopatra. I always tell my groups to expect the unexpected, but I warn more about the hardships of traveling in a third world country, getting accustomed to a new diet, and feeling comfortable around hordes of children crying, "Baksheesh, baksheesh," which means, "Give me money." When you go to Egypt, go without expectations. See and feel and absorb what you can in this strange but beckoning vortex of spiritual beauty.

Our groups meditate to synthesize our energies to ancient events and thought impressions, or sit in a cool spot in a temple and discuss the mythology of that sacred spot. Like Sedona, Egypt will open your mind and force you to face unresolved issues. I had an unpleasant experience once with a woman traveler when her male side drew swords with my feminine shadow. I had been assigned a special room at the Mena House overlooking the Great Pyramid, and she felt entitled to it. The misunderstanding was settled when the manager explained that the room was only suitable for one person and the woman had a roommate. My softer side mediated a peaceful settlement by inviting her to my room one afternoon for tea.

Thousands of people have sensed that Egypt prepared them to face a divorce, make a career change, or heal a broken relationship with a loved one—and each in his or her own way describes the experience generally along the same lines: "Something, some energy or thought impression when I was in the Valley of the Kings (or in Abu Simbel or Dendera or the Egyptian Museum) gave me divine guidance that was real and unequivocal. It exceeded vivid imagination."

I have come to believe that it is the silent and invisible worlds that are more life-changing than logic and reason or what we can see and touch. These Egyptian phenomena remind me of the Kierkegaardian *blind leap of faith.*

Travelers to Egypt have the best time if they bring their well-mannered inner child along for the journey. I remember to pack a healthy sense of humor before I leave home.

What I pray happens to each of us is that we open ourselves to the melodies of the setting sun and the resurgence at daybreak of the adventures that can lead to psychic change—to rediscover the forgotten true self. Before we leave the sand and sounds of Aton Ra and Ramses, I wish for everyone to find a deep and abiding peace that echoes through the Valley of the Kings and Queens.

INITIATION INTO THE LIGHT

An initiation in the Great Pyramid is a simple but stirring ceremony. Each initiate lies down in a sarcophagus, in a crypt built for a royal mummy carved from limestone. This coffin in the Great Pyramid once held the body of King Cheops, the second pharaoh of the Fourth Dynasty of the Old Kingdom of Egypt. The initiate crosses his arms over his chest and crystals are placed on his seven chakras, or energy centers, on his body. The Initiator chants and intones whatever he or she intuits for the initiate, inducing a trance state that continues throughout the initiation. The ceremony lasts about thirty minutes.

When I was initiated in 1983 I was able to hear the word "Toulouse"—the name of a town in France—repeated over and over again. Within three years I took a Grail Quest (the phrase Grail Quest has come to mean seeking the answer to the question, "Who am I?") which began in Toulouse, the linchpin of *Holy Blood, Holy Grail* by Michael Baigent, Richard Leigh, and Henry Lincoln, which was first published around the time of my first trek to Egypt. Toulouse is reported to be the starting point for a Grail Quest. Authorities and historians who study what the Grail means and guide students on the journey through the Pyrenees believe the trek starts in Toulouse. I saw a series of events that have come to pass, a confirmation of having started the Sedona Intensive, writing books, and speaking before large crowds. I was "told" mind-to-mind from a guided source that this assignment to come to Egypt time and time again and to bring others brought me closer to my own redemption from darkness into light. I understood I would have a permanent connection to my true self and that I must do the things to maintain this enlightenment which I have suggested to you in this chapter.

I have been to Egypt nine times, dating from 1983. With each journey another Albert, perhaps more the real me each time, was synchronistically coming into being, and not only through my initiation inside the Great Pyramid but also astrologically. It was time to let go of the people-pleasing, accommodating person I had always been. With this cognition came an overwhelming desire to leave these people with whom I had been touring and get away from their rituals. I had come here to reconnect with Egypt's energies, not to talk endlessly about what prophecies each person received. One person said, "I am sure that I was Hatshepsut." And another declared, "I was Ramses II." My time there was about the inner journey, not show-and-tell.

THERE ARE NO COINCIDENCES

On this trip, I was told that a woman from another tour group wanted to meet with me and she invited me to have high tea with her. She had watched from across the dining room as our group celebrated my birthday and was amused at my surprised responses as I opened every present. She later said that there was something about my energy that piqued her interest—she wanted to know me up close.

As I rested before my tea date, I once more drifted immediately to that reservoir of information where truth lies. And once again I heard the powerful message: *Out of the darkness and into the light.*

I lay still for a moment to process the information I had accessed. As Paul promised earlier, the mention of the word light made me feel more centered, more hopeful, and more connected to a power greater than me. I sat up to get ready for my rendezvous feeling weightless, but centered within myself.

I walked through the open door onto a deck shaded by a green and white striped canopy, with matching cushioned deck chairs and tiny café tables. She was seated in profile and wearing smoked eyeglasses. She was dressed in a beige twill suit with a black-patterned Hermès scarf around her shoulders, and she wore little jewelry.

The wind was up, carrying a light spray from the river.

The boat moved slowly toward the heart of Luxor, where the cruise would end for her.

I tiptoed toward her. I suspected she was catnapping.

"Madame Sadat, I am Albert Gaulden," I stated rather formally.

"Oh, sorry, you gave me a start," Jehan Sadat said. "Please, sit here."

She motioned me to a chair to her right. I turned it slightly so I could see her better.

"Your tour operator tells me that you talk a lot about my husband, Anwar," she said with the trace of a smile.

"I speak of him often because no one has ever touched me like he did. At a time when Egypt was at her most vulnerable from dissidents, President Sadat showed courage and character. When he died, I grieved as one would for a father. I call him Egypt's brightest light."

Madame Jehan Sadat was quiet, gazing into my eyes. A long time passed before either of us spoke.

On October 6, 1981, Egyptian President Anwar el-Sadat was assassinated as he watched a military review celebrating the reclamation of lands from Israel. I had been staying at the Regency Hotel in New York in 1978 when he, Menachem Begin, and President Jimmy Carter got off the elevator in front of me. They had been drafting peace accords. Sadat's piercing gaze into my eyes was like a lightning bolt to my nervous system. Although we never met, that look registered something in me—we connected without words.

That year I wrote a screenplay, *The World Is Waiting*, which ends in a peace festival in Cairo. A producer-partner arranged for us to meet with President Sadat in November 1981 to discuss filming in Egypt. He died the month before.

"Anwar was for all people. He believed more than anyone in peace in the Middle East," Madame Sadat said quietly.

Paul's voice played in my head: *Man loves darkness rather than light.*

A butler poured tea, and we drank and talked for more than an hour. I told her about seeing her husband in New York with Begin and Carter, and about the meeting for my movie that was not to be.

"What incredible coincidences. What are the odds that you and I would meet?" she asked.

"There are no coincidences, Madame Sadat. We meet people that we need to know, which is known as synchronicity," I said.

"Albert, who are you? What do you know and how do you know it?" she asked.

"Madame Sadat, I don't know how to answer that question. Peculiar things have been happening to me lately to change my perception of me and the world. This

I do know: none of us is who we think we are, and things are not what they seem," I said.

We stared at the feluccas drifting by and waved to the workers tending their sails. Madame Sadat seemed to be processing what I had said.

"Tell me more about coincidences. They puzzle me," she said. Madame Sadat leaned in very close to my face and asked, "Do you think that Anwar's death was a struggle between good and evil or simply God's plan?" she asked.

I cleared my throat and paused to collect my thoughts. I knew that she knew the answer, but I still needed to measure my words.

I took both her hands and held them for a moment and then said, "You asked me two things. As far as coincidences are concerned, there are no coincidences and there are no accidents, including our meeting this afternoon. Everything we do and everything that happens to us, including the bad stuff, is by divine design; everything is preplanned, albeit we have free will. My intuition tells me that the death of President Sadat was both a struggle with the dark side and God's will. President Sadat's death was karmic."

She closed her eyes and sat silhouetted by the setting sun. A sudden chill caused her to pull the oversized scarf more tightly around her shoulders.

"Why do you come here so often? What so fascinates you with this country?" she asked.

"Sedona, Arizona, where I live, and Egypt are similar. As I watch the landscape along the Nile, I am reminded of Sedona. Sedona is known as Red Rock Country, because she is nestled in a valley of craggy reddish-brown sandstone formations millions of years old. If you look closely, hundreds of etched figures appear to stand guard over the small community below. I see the same faces in the mountains of sand and limestone here in Egypt."

I explained about Sedona's energy centers and what people report experiencing there.

"Hopi elders say that the Indians from Arizona migrated from Egypt. Egypt draws me here, just as Sedona lures travelers to meditate and feel her transcendent vortexes. Your people are my people and my people are your people. We gather along the mystical Nile for reunion," I said.

I learned more about my adopted country from one who knew it well. Madame Sadat smiled when I spoke of Egypt's children and women and how both must be better schooled and protected.

"I feel as you do, Albert. The Egyptian woman is oppressed. The women here need better education and equal career opportunities with men. Egypt in many ways still lives in the dark ages," she said.

As I started to leave, she grabbed my hand and held it for a moment. "Thank you for speaking to me about Anwar. I always like to hear how people everywhere love him."

"I hope that you do not think me presumptuous, but I feel that you and President Sadat are twin flames. You both hold a strong light for others. When I look at you, I see him. You are the same. His light, your light, will never fail."

She nodded with closed eyes.

I stood to leave. My group was peeking around the door from the lounge. I motioned to them, and like children excited and thrilled to be meeting such a famous lady, they came out quickly and I introduced each one.

As we left, I turned back and said, "Madame Sadat, Anwar did not die. He lives. I feel him, I see him with us now. He will affect the world for a long, long time. Thank you for courage to speak as you do here and in America and all over the planet about what needs to change in Egypt and the world."

Jehan Sadat smiled and nodded. Then she turned her head back toward the land we were leaving. I knew she wanted to be alone, and I left.

Dusk in Egypt is an eerie but magical tableau photographed time and again for travel magazines. Sounds and smells and swirling dust conjure memories of dynasties and deities who once ruled this strange and mystical sandbox.

As darkness descended toward the horizon, I could see the faint outline of Madame Sadat as she climbed the limestone steps to the boulevard above. At street level she looked toward the boat, and I waved. Jehan Sadat stepped into a car, and was gone.

I sat on the deck alone for most of the night. Around two o'clock in the morning I grabbed a couple of blankets from a stack on a nearby table. I was drifting, floating, sleeping, and dreaming. Paul soon came to tuck me in and hold me in God's grace as he repeated, *"Out of the darkness and into the light."*

THE LIGHT LEADS US

The next morning, the captain rang my room and asked me to pack my luggage—he was moving me. He would come to get me in a few minutes. We walked down the corridor on the lower floor and stopped at door 201. He opened it and we entered a suite with a sweeping view of the countryside disappearing behind the boat in muted blues, purples, and greens.

"This is Madame Sadat's suite. She designed this room. You are standing on an antique rug that has been in her family for centuries. This is her furniture, her antiques and tapestries. She asked that you stay here until you leave the boat in three days. If you need anything, please call me personally. Madame Sadat said for us to care for you as we do her," the captain said. He handed me the key.

I sat down dumbstruck. I am in her suite, I said to

myself. This was over the rainbow. The bedroom was large enough to accommodate a king-sized bed with an antique gold-inlay headboard. I pulled back the patterned blue-green bedspread and found embroidered Egyptian cotton sheets and pillowcases.

On the bedside table was a letter for me on her personal note paper.

> Mr. Albert: Thank you for such a wonderful afternoon tea. It pleases me how long and how much you have loved my husband. I hope you enjoy this room as much as I do. You will find it conducive to write, but most of all, to be alone with your thoughts about your favorite country in the world. We have something in common: I love America as much as you love my Egypt. Have a wonderful time in mystical Egypt.
> Fond wishes,
> Jehan Sadat

I moved around the suite, touching everything to see if anything stimulated my intuition. There was a separate sitting room with a chintz sofa and two matching chairs. Oil paintings and watercolors of the Impressionist period hung on the walls. End tables, Persian rugs, and an antique armoire finished the appointments. A mini-bar was stocked with sodas, champagne, fruit juices, and mineral water.

The marble bathroom had faux-gold fixtures, a large Jacuzzi bathtub, and a separate spacious shower. The bath sheets were thick and fluffy. The soaps, shampoos, and perfumes were from Paris.

I called for my luggage. I unpacked, drew a bath, and took a long and relaxing meditation in the royal tub. It was the perfect preparation for writing in my journal. "If you don't keep track of where you've been, you'll never know where you're going," my spiritual teacher told me.

My entry was interesting as much for what followed as for what I wrote:

"I'm sitting here in Madame Sadat's suite feeling like royalty. I'm thinking how strange it is to feel more connected to acquaintances, travelers, and clients than I do to my family. Why would I rather travel with ten people I don't know than with my mother or brothers and sisters?"

I needed to investigate karma and my family.

CHAPTER 5

Stage Four—Karmic Mirrors

Stage Four is a lesson in karma. The concept of the karmic mirror is a simple one. In order to retrieve, shift back to, who we really are—the one created by the Divine—we must feel what others abused by us in past lives and in this one have endured and how they have been harmed; they must do to us what we have done to them so that we will see how it feels and be soul-shocked into seeking redemption. Karma is simply facing those things we have done which were initiated by our ego in contradiction to what the soul urge of our true self would have us do.

Our families are karmic mirrors. What we have come back to Earth to learn is in the family circle. None of us is born into a family by accident. Everything has been pre-arranged. We pick a family whose karma fits our own.

Seeing our parents as who they truly are—their good qualities as well as their character defects—exposes what we need to look at within ourselves. We are our parents. What you dislike or disapprove of in a parent are qualities that you yourself had in a previous life. You have come back hypersensitive to these characteristics. The secret to wholeness is to see them mirrored so they can be corrected within you.

Swami once asked me, "Some people see only the good in all of us and believe their parents are perfect. What would you say about them?"

"I think they are in denial," I answered.

As much as I like to see what's good in me or anyone else, I have to keep digging until I get to what drove me and them back here to the Lower World to face past misdeeds.

Everything we have learned and continue to learn is tied to paradox. It is all about me—looking at my part in what went wrong in all areas of my life instead of blaming others—but it is also all about all of us. Life is repertory theatre; each of us plays a part to teach and learn important lessons.

We can change patterns of dysfunction in the family by exposing secrets and healing emotional pain.

MY FAMILY

I was nine years old when my parents divorced.

As I mentioned before, Dad was an undependable father who never kept promises. Ty Gaulden was a drunk, a rogue, a famous philanderer who married six times, and also a kid at heart, who could flatter a turtle from its shell and make you laugh or cry, depending on his mood. He was also a semiprofessional baseball player whom his teammates nicknamed Ty, after Ty Cobb, the legendary "Georgia Peach" who played for the Detroit Tigers (1905–1926). After a brief period of success in baseball, he was forced to accept the harsh reality of being a laborer, working in the steel mills—sweaty and dirty. Dad was an irresponsible father to us kids and a two-timing husband to his women. He died blind and consumed by cancer in 1980.

My mother Maggie was a willing victim who worked as a file clerk yet raised six children in a housing project. Maggie was beautiful and bold. She could also be mean and crazy. The craziness sprang from not wanting to be a mother, no matter how much she told everyone that her children were her life. My mother felt trapped. She wanted a life without her children, but there was nothing she could do but sacrifice everything for us kids. When confronted with anything she didn't want to face, Maggie would dig a hole and hide. Not a drinker, she was a devotee of God, and she was always fiscally responsible.

I saw her as she was, and I would eventually see myself in her.

I have three sisters and two brothers who divided into two opposing camps when we were growing up. The two sides could have belonged to different families. Shame-based, but honest and diligent, all my siblings knew their place in the world and stayed there. I didn't. I still don't and never will.

When I got sober I called my dad on the telephone to make amends. I asked him to forgive me for being a selfish, unloving son, for never calling him or remembering his birthday with a call or a card. I was amazed at how like him I was. We were both alcoholics, rambling roses, with hair-trigger tempers.

Daddy always called his sons "boy," even after Bill, Hank, and I were over forty. I'll never forget that telephone conversation on April 28, 1980:

"Boy, you were always your daddy's favorite. Where did you get that I was ashamed of you?"

"I thought it was because I didn't play sports like Bill and Hank."

Daddy had coached baseball all his adult life. At the time of his death he was chairman emeritus of Little Boys' Baseball, an organization that racist white men in the South put together when Little League was forced by law to integrate.

"Anybody can play sports, boy. God didn't mean for

you to be an athlete, else you wouldn't have been born with club feet. God wanted you to use your mind. Be a teacher or a writer. Hell, boy, I named you after me even though Bill was the oldest. You and I are the same: rip-roaring, hell-raising drunks."

My dad died the day after I made amends to him. We traveled the same back roads, got into the same kinds of trouble with the law, and had the same misguided zest for living. Today I love my daddy and I miss him.

Mother's quintessential attributes of perseverance and determination rubbed off on me more after recovery than when I was growing up. Mom was a perfectionist and always asked questions to see how something could be done better. I inherited that trait as well. We have not always been the most popular, but like her, I fall asleep when my head hits the pillow. Mother was always my best friend, even when I didn't think so. Not a day goes by that I don't miss her and wish that we had had more time together.

THE FAMILY PHONIES

There is no better place to see how and why you are a big phony—as inauthentic as they come (the prover-bial "bad penny")—than the family scrapbook, or as we call it in our family, a trip down memory lane. Hiding in plain sight in the photo album are the goblins and ghosts—the chamber of horrors—of childhood and beyond. Perhaps these hypotheticals ring true for you. On the first page is daddy, the town drunk and wife beater. Remember all the Christmases when you thought it was so funny when he fell into the tree or came home with bad company to spoil the holiday for everyone? We're not just talking about trailer trash here. Craziness lives in the big house on the hill as well as on the wrong side of the tracks. Remember Mamma—she could put on a good front with company and be mean as a snake when she was the disciplinarian? Oh, there's Aunt Thelma before she chased her kids out the door waving a knife and screaming, "I'll kill you when I catch you." That was right after she got home from Sunday school and church.

The dirty rotten shame of this journey back through the family timeline is that your parents and siblings and grandparents—and aunts and uncles and cousins—are not who you think they are. The reason all of us, family members included, act like we do—drinking and overeating and addicted to sex, drugs, and rock and roll is that we are sick and tired of living a life we can't stand. I always say, "Thank God I found booze instead of the ministry," because repressing all those anti-Jesus feelings and trying to be a good little boy drove me nuts. I needed to tear my world apart so God could help it fall into place. Being dead broke and down and out beat living a lie, until I decided to stop burying the real me with addictions and compulsions. Many of us need a stiff shot of whiskey and another piece of pie or another run-away-from-home-vacation to escape the false us.

You can try to clean up the rap sheet of all the nasty mean fights and the unhealthy accusations one member of the mob made to another, but it always comes back to the same cracked mirror of karma: nobody was taking responsibility for his actions; nobody blew the whistle on the cover-up and said, "I am not playing this game anymore." Not one single twisted soul copped a plea to his shameful conduct and I'll bet my last nickel there were no amends. No one dared say, "It's my fault and I want to make amends for my behavior."

There are those of us who have a much better replay of our life growing up. Many of us have loving and supportive parents, siblings, and other relatives who are kind and considerate. I have many friends and clients who make the most of the hand life dealt them, but there are no perfect families and there are no Snow Whites in the sisterhood. The family circle can be nurturing and hands-on, but there are learning curves in the best of Good Housekeeping–approved family units.

ACCEPTING YOUR FAMILY'S KARMA

Taking stock of your life history means writing down your earliest memories of important events, especially traumas and major upsets, and describing your response to them. The life history I took in my first days of sobriety convinced me that I was switched at birth. I snarled, "Those people, my family, are nothing like me and I am certainly not acting out from their gene pool." Yet when I accept the rules of karma, I realize there are pieces of them in me, and I love my family and accept the part of me that is them. It was through personal discovery, by taking a hard look at my inner landscape, that I began to change. Loving the bad in my dad and the unacceptable in mom helped me forgive and love myself.

Nine generations of the men in the Gaulden family had been alcoholics, and I would follow. But Daddy and I cleaned up the Gaulden bloodline when we sobered up. My brothers and sisters don't drink. I turned out to be supercritical, never believing that anything was ever good enough—a major flaw in my mother and her family. Through my inventory and later in my practice, I had to cultivate patience and tolerance much as a gymnast would develop his muscles. I finally faced the truth that I am my picky, critical, and analytical mother and I am my alcoholic, sex-addicted father. My brothers and sisters taught me more humility than I would have learned in an orphanage. I cast them in the play I wrote to help me look at me.

Once again, it's karma. If I don't see the changes I need to make, I will return again and again to face what I refused to look at in this life. The conditions will get rougher and tougher in each subsequent life. I am the friends and well-known people I admire, and the ones I can't stand and judge as well. When I clear away false perceptions of who I am and live consciously daily, I clear away lifetimes of how I have misidentified myself. I Windex the family karmic mirror clean.

In William Shakespeare's *As You Like It,* he writes, "All the world's a stage...." He suggests that the roles are somewhat beyond the players' control and that the script for the play has already been written by an eternal power. If all of us are actors in the plays we write, could it be that we are in repertory theatre, first acting the part of the child and then the part of the parent, in a subsequent life? Who am I to disagree with Shakespeare, but I myself believe in free will. When you get the message, start changing what you can—you. The notion that the stage has been set and everyone has his script makes sense, if we understand that we are here to rewrite scene after scene with an altered consciousness and right use of will.

All of this suggests that perhaps you *have been* your mother and father and siblings in a previous incarnation. At the very least, if you want to know what lessons you need to learn and who your teachers are, look at those seated around the dinner table. All of us are interrelated through karma and ancestrally to our family members, and those we like least will force us to look at our own hidden parts contained in their dark side. What you don't like about your mother is what you find unacceptable in yourself. If you find a lot to abhor in your father, the seed of discontent is to be found within you.

Some of us make a decision to pick up our purse and leave or pack up at a young age and get the hell out of Dodge. Our father's drunkenness embarrasses us or our mother's promiscuity repulses us. Our siblings are hooked on drugs or get pregnant with no means of supporting a child and nowhere to live. We label them trailer trash and want nothing to do with them. Running away seems a smart way to distance ourselves from these low-lifes, users, and abusers.

To my way of thinking, this is avoidance. We are born to a mother and father and have siblings to learn lessons, work off karma, and restore our souls to their righteous and holy condition. Pain and suffering don't discriminate—sexual abuse and shoddy parenting happen on Park Avenue as well as Tobacco Road.

Stay the course. Learn your lessons. You can make a difference if your own house is in order. Be direct. Get professional help. Call in the cavalry—professional interventionists and therapists. Call a twelve-step hotline and start sorting dirty laundry. Don't run. My High Self tells me if I look the other way or cut and run I will come back and have to face these deep-seated issues in another life.

LOOKING IN THE KARMIC MIRROR

There are no victims in the family chamber of horrors. Whatever your lot—unloving parents, being born into poverty—you deserved it. Natural law demands that you feel what it felt like to inflict something on someone else. You must experience *every single thing* you've ever done to harm another. This is karmic retribution.

You need look no farther than the family tree to know what you have to clear. If daddy's a drunk, check your tolerance for alcohol. It is important to look at all addictions and compulsions.

Where do you look for what's wrong with whom—and how to change? Look at nutty Uncle Eddie's antics. See momma as flawed but doing the best she can—and make a vow not to live out her defects. Don't try to become her. Be you—the real you. Stare at your brother and sister until you get an eyeful of family dysfunction and toxicity. Lie, cheat, steal, and deny it all, but you'll see yourself and what you need to change by looking in the karmic mirror. Change starts with forgiving yourself and then making amends with those you have hurt.

If Uncle Joe dies in a car wreck, more than likely he

killed someone in another life. It may have been a chariot or a covered wagon, but Joe took a life, and now has to experience having his life ended by someone else. Many of us question why bad things happen to good people. Aunt Mildred never harmed a fly. So why was she raped and murdered? I believe that in a former existence, she raped and murdered someone herself.

What do you see when you look, and what do you hear when you listen? See a victim and you will become one. See a precious child of God and you'll do what you need to do to become again who God created you to be. Hear yourself enumerating what's bad about life and how everybody's always picking on you and you'll never turn up the volume to God's divine plan for your life. The movie you're in is trying to show you the litany of what you've done that needs major transformation. There are no mistakes; it's show time.

DNA swears we will look like our parents at seventy, contract their diseases, lose the same amount of hair, and even embrace their habits. In the silent and invisible Upper World of supreme authority, there is a holy principle of action and reaction. If you inherited your daddy's eyes, why wouldn't you catch his laziness? If momma mistreated you, could you have been a bad mother somewhere in time?

You do not necessarily inherit all the bad or good qualities of your family. You don't become an alcoholic just because your father is, but mother and father and everybody else you are related to have other qualities that are just as destructive, like womanizing or gambling, or you may have inherited a propensity for physical or sexual abuse. Children always share in their parents' karma. We can't blame our family for the way we turn out, but we need to make a vow to change the lineage. My dad and I sobered up, the first in that ancestral tree for more than a hundred years.

And I would be remiss not to mention that you might have been gifted with all the good qualities from mom and dad and grandparents like unselfishness, kindness, being nurturing, and being temperate in all areas of life.

What can you do about family dysfunction? Here's my checklist:

1. Determine to get help. Everybody's sick somewhere. Oftentimes, it can be as simple as working with a life coach. In other cases, you may want to hire a licensed psychologist or transpersonal therapist. Well people are in therapy; sick people are in denial.
2. Take a fearless and moral inventory of family secrets. It will show you where the golden aspects of the family lie as well as uncover all the scary aspects of betrayal and distrust.
3. Resign from the debating society and stop the blame

game. Look at yourself and work on you. Don't baby-sit or baby talk mom's sickness and don't carry a brother's shame.

4. Be direct. Speak truthfully and don't permit yourself or anyone else to candy-coat hurt deeds or harsh words.

5. Determine to be the family member who's come to the end of the line with family bizarre behavior and inappropriate treatment of yourself and them. Change you and clear you of this never ending chaos.

I remember a client who had been born out of wedlock. Her mother married soon after she was born, and the new husband took the baby as his own. It was never discussed until my client, June, came to Sedona to work with me.

When she wrote about family secrets, June revealed that her mother was not married when she was born. June agonized over the big lie and secret for more than thirty years. Telling me freed her from the prison of shame.

I had her speak to her mother when she returned home. She let her mother know that she loved her and her father, but that she wanted to be free of secrets. The communication opened locked doors of guilt, fear, shame, and misunderstanding. And it elicited an admission by her mother that she had secretly hated June and wished that June had never been born. June also found out that her grandmother had borne a child out of wed-lock: her own mother. June and her mother had a glorious homecoming because one of them refused to live a lie. June faced an ego that tried to make her live a life full of fear and separation, and her ego lost.

In my brand of therapy, I have clients write themselves out of dark and dangerous places. The mind is a favorite lodge for egocentric misinformation. Stinking thinking prevents you from open and honest review.

I studied under a spiritual teacher who said that past misdeeds are caked and layered in our subconscious. He used the analogy of someone waxing a dirty floor without cleaning the dirt and grime before applying the polish. The surface shines, but what lies beneath is filth.

Changing the things we can starts with making direct amends to those we have harmed. Do not live your life riddled with resentments. All parties are at fault. No one is the sole culprit. Asking forgiveness for your part in a disagreement or an all-out catfight or worse will free you.

After the unpleasant business has been cleaned and cleared, practice whatever steps or daily remedies you need to stay that way. That will lead you to the next lesson.

CHAPTER 6

Stage Five—You're Not Who You Think You Are

Gender and the body in which your physical being was born have predetermined many of your experiences on this Earth.

But in Stage Five, you will come to understand and be willing to accept that you're not who you think you are, and things are not what they seem.

Carl Jung discovered that within every man is the reflection of a woman and within every woman is the reflection of a man. Jung called this reflection one's shadow. Dr. John A. Sanford, a Jungian therapist, referred to this ignored side of a person as the "invisible partner." In *The*

Invisible Partners: How the Male and Female in Each of Us Affects Our Relationships, Dr. Sanford says that if we refuse to recognize the invisible partner (or shadow), it can drive us to drink excessively, act out adulterously, and even commit murder.

When I was enlightened to the concept of the shadow and how it represents the spirit of the feminine within me and the masculine within women, I felt liberation. This shadow or invisible partner is the one with whom I must make peace and come into balance in order to have healthy and loving relationships with all people, but especially with someone whom I love and with whom I want to spend my life.

Gender is part mask, and without integration of the shadow, we will continue to live half a life. The Adam and Eve biblical fable—God creating Eve from Adam's rib—is an interesting twist on how the split happened. Reconnecting to the light of the Creator, I can access historical memory of spiritual holism through gender assimilation.

Parents, teachers, and peer groups have identified us through their own bias. Rather than being the son or daughter of our parents, we are the sons and daughters of God—macrocosmic and microcosmic—returning to Earth on assignment to clear up the past and to help others do the same. And it is only as a male united with my inner feminine personality that I can do what I came back to do.

I am man and woman. My true partner is within me. For millennia and lifetimes I have been looking for a partner to make me happy, but I can only find joy within myself, and then, if it be God's will, I can have a partner outside myself.

Knowing that I am not who I think I am is freeing. I never felt like I belonged, whether at home, in my community, or at school, and rarely did I feel that friends and acquaintances were who they thought they were. I am becoming; I am unfolding, and I am remembering who I am.

We are all powerful light beings who have lost the middle ground, the psychological androgyny of consciousness, by reincarnating as a man and then a woman, changing gender randomly from one lifetime to another. But in truth we are neither male nor female—we are both.

YOUR INVISIBLE PARTNER OR SHADOW

We can define the invisible partner in simpler language. The spirit of the invisible partner within the man acts like any ordinary woman, except that she can be heard by everyone except the man in whom she lives. The shadow wants to be able to participate in a man's life and when denied that privilege, she will act out like a spoiled child, or worse. She can cause the man to slip into a foul mood.

He starts to complain and find fault with everything and everybody—it's as if he is possessed by a witch.

The shadow never likes to be taken for granted or ignored. This sounds as if the shadow is more trouble than it's worth—but only when we transfer, or project, our negative and unattractive qualities onto someone else. We need to face what the shadow is trying to teach us about ourselves that needs to be changed. When we blame our mother for not having been born richer, that is a form of transference. Rather than accept the hand life dealt us, we pass our inadequacies off onto mama. A woman throws her suspicions of infidelity onto her lover or husband without any grounds or concrete facts of relationship misconduct. It is her own desire to get into a clandestine affair which triggers her need to blame her mate. The shadow is the master therapist who can lead you into peace, balance, and harmony through a synthesis of shadow and self, when you let it.

The same applies for women. Liken this relationship to a puppet, the woman, having her strings tugged, and a puppeteer, the shadow, pulling the strings. The shadow will drive a woman to scream and rage at and blame her mate as a way to get the woman to realize that she is unhappy with herself; the partner may or may not be blameless.

The shadow is saying to her: "Look at you. You are getting mad at the wrong person. He's just being the man you attracted to you so you could bottom out with all your bad-girl behavior. Bond with me; let's you and I have a relationship so you can make peace with yourself. I can help you put an end to this insanity and correct these never-ending defects in relationships."

It's like the shadow is getting her to act out so she can observe her lunacy. Whenever she gets disturbed and overreacts with a partner, she is the one at fault, because she is the one raging. The fulcrum of her outburst could be pent up anger at a father or the bad blood between her and an ex-husband or an old lover. She has buried these feelings, and the shadow needles her and cajoles her to act out, as a way to get her to face the real problem. She is raging at her lover when it is her father whom she would like to strangle.

Her shadow is trying to help her first to survive and then to grow up emotionally by digging deep within herself until she reaches all the anger, resentment, blame, shame, and every other buried feeling that has caused her to lose at having a relationship with herself or someone else. She needs to look at the source of these feelings and heal them. Her shadow does not want her to be dependent on a man for her happiness. But she will never become independent until she gets acquainted with her invisible partner.

I suggest to my clients that they name their invisible partners and talk out loud to them. This may seem a bit weird at first, but before long it sinks in that you and your shadow are one and the same—you live the part of one gender, and the shadow represents your opposite-gender side. If you have never talked to yourself, you are missing out on one of life's greatest pleasures. The more you engage and dialogue with your shadow, the less dependent you are going to be on your spouse or lover or anyone else for that matter. This is an effective exercise to let go of somebody else's garbage and, at the same time, tend to your own stinking thinking.

You: "Since my name is Mary, may I call you Marcus?"

Shadow: "I prefer Marco—I am an Italian."

You: "I need some help from you, Marco. Why do my husband and I fight all the time?"

Shadow: "You want something from him that only I can give you."

You: "What?"

Shadow: "You are angry that you are both advertising executives but he makes more money than you do. Am I right?"

You: "Yes. And he is not as smart as I am."

Shadow: "Prove your worth to your boss at work. Don't take it out on your husband at home."

You: "How can I get rid of this anger toward my husband?"

Shadow: "Have a weekly powwow where you both get everything off your chests and out in the open, where you can discuss troubling issues and resolve hidden resentments. If you do this, your resentments will disappear and you will remember the real reasons you married your husband in the first place."

By being honest with yourself, you are resolving many of the key issues in your marriage or with your partner. These kinds of chats with our shadow are how many of us learn to distinguish between what we can change and what we must accept in the other. We can only change us.

The invisible partner can either be ignored or integrated. In order to become whole you must embrace your ego, for ego and the shadow are synonymous— they are the same troublemakers. When you make the shadow a friend, it becomes an ally in balancing your internal world.

Because we are unaware of this unseen personality, we don't know to get acquainted with our shadow. Instead we unconsciously project the shadow onto the one we love, and that transference breeds contempt. We deny that a quality like jealousy or passive-aggressive behavior is ours, so we convince ourselves that these unattractive character defects describe the other person. I suggest you talk and talk and talk to your shadow until you get good positive results from the collaboration.

YOUR SHADOW AND YOUR RELATIONSHIPS

From the moment you landed on planet Earth, nobody had a clue about who you were. You were mislabeled at birth. Dress boys in blue, girls in pink? I don't think so.

Your parents are not who you think they are either. Husbands, wives, and lovers are everything and anything but who you think they are. All of us create the other from our own egocentric points of view. Yet it goes deeper and deadlier than that: We need someone to inherit the unwanted, unattractive qualities within us that we refuse to face and heal.

Unfortunately, it doesn't work that way. When we play the blame game, accusing our lovers for why we feel bad, they should say to us, "Deal with your own anger—let me deal with my own issues." The problem is that few of us are throwing stuff back to the other side of the fence where it belongs.

Before you can embrace the notion of following the light with the help of spirit guidance, you must look at the practical, feet-on-the-ground truth about what blocks you from being who God created you to be.

A split the size of the Grand Canyon has existed for so long between men and women. The great divide is not what you're fighting over—money, property, or who gets the bigger closet. The schism that occurs in love, courtship, and marriage has to do with a failure of both partners to love, touch, feel, hold, and nurture a key relationship: the relationship with oneself. This is the partnership that can free you from the treadmill of picking the same disastrous lover over and over again.

I had a Gentle Ben client named Mike who was married to Misty, a woman who was all Victoria's Secret and *Desperate Housewives,* until her masculine side acted up. Then Misty became more of a man than Mike.

Misty had low self-esteem, hated her father, and thought her mom was a doormat. She jogged five miles a day, took aerobics and yoga classes, excelled in martial arts, read self-help books, and nagged Mike to attend countless lectures on relationships. But nothing ever got better with Mike and Misty. They blamed each other for what didn't work and never saw their own part in what was wrong with their marriage.

Mike had a dictator for a daddy. Nothing Mike ever did was good enough. Mike's mom was schizophrenic and died when he was young. Finding the right woman became an obsession for him, for he needed someone soft, soothing, and tender to tell him he was okay.

Where did the marriage break down? Mike never found a woman to replace his mother. A wife is not a mother and can never heal what a mother couldn't or didn't do. His passive-aggressive behavior was masking his fear of confronting what was wrong with him.

If Misty didn't like her father, she wasn't going to find a husband to make her happy. She was unconsciously running old tapes that affected how she felt about men generally. And plastic surgery never healed soul sickness.

But a good, honest inventory of our character flaws, including past wrongs to others, can do wonders to heal what hurts and to save ourselves and our relationship.

How could the relationship between Mike and Misty have healed and gotten better? He could have acknowledged that he needed to make friends with his shadow, whom I referred to as "Christine" in our therapy, rather than continue to look for a woman to fix him, and he could have confessed how he used people, places, and things to deaden the pain of how unloved he felt. And he could have been honest with Misty that he didn't know how to have a relationship. Misty could have begun the healing process by changing her inner life through prayer, meditation, and keeping a journal which in turn would fix her outer world. She could have turned inward to engage her masculine side, whom we named Milos. Such a relationship would have helped her heal her daddy issues. Once we wake up to what we are doing and recognize that our irritations are about us and not someone else, we can no longer project our unattractive, unwanted negative qualities onto our significant relationships. Projections are always unconscious. When you become conscious, you must face what's wrong with you.

One of the major reasons we are not able to make a partnership work is that these projected qualities keep getting in the way of peaceful coexistence. The shadow has caused trouble since the time of Adam and Eve because it wants to be recognized, to be a part of our lives, to become integrated into our outward personality, but it is almost always ignored. It wants to save us, but we won't let it.

Who among us has ever been told to value his dark side? Who among us has ever acknowledged the sheer power of the sinister underbelly of his soul? Who of us has ever realized that he can't have a relationship with someone else because he has never had one with all of himself? Let the shadow tell you about your own shortcomings, so that you can amend them. Permit the shadow to take you to scary places where you will not like what you see. In a moment of clarity, your true self will trump your false identity as a result of looking more honestly at yourself. My dark side teaches me more than all the hot lights of Heaven. The shadow will drive you to look at your bondage, but will allow you to reunite the High Self which will liberate you.

YOU'RE STRAIGHT? WELL, YOU'RE ALSO GAY

"Is she gay or isn't she?" "Is he gay or isn't he?" These questions have a life of their own. Curiosity about someone else's sexuality really points to questions you have about your own sexual identity. And nowhere is this more apparent than in Hollywood where everyone is always trying to figure out if this actor prefers men, or that actress likes women. Within the middle ground where androgyny lives, we can find answers to confusion about "Am I or am I not?"

Major cities and small towns are full of married men and women who have a same-sex lover on the side. Oprah Winfrey did a television show called "Living on the Down Low," about this very topic: men who have sex with other men but keep their wives and girlfriends for appearances—to make them look straight. I wish I had a dime for all the straight men I have worked with who have had sex with another man—one-night, two-night, a-lot-of-night stands. These men run into one another in dark parks and seedy bars, and at exclusive country clubs.

Gary J. Gates, a demographer at the Williams Institute, a UCLA research group that studies gay issues, found that as high as 38 percent of gay men have been married. Of 27 million married men, Mr. Gates found that 1.6 percent, or 436,000, said they were gay or bisexual. He cites Cole Porter and former governor of New Jersey James McGreevey as men who were married and yet had relationships with a man or men on the side.

Much of this behavior stems from the homophobic

society we are raised in. As long as fathers keep trying to make their sons into stud athletes and moms insist their daughters act and dress like beauty queens, the imbalance is going to create more closeted kids who grow up afraid to express their sexual desires no matter what they might be.

Gender studies are proliferating in colleges and universities around the country, instigated by young people dying to know who they are and how to express themselves in sexual relationships or fantasies. They seem to be saying to all of us, "Wait a minute: something about what I have been taught about my sexual identity doesn't compute. Something *is* rotten in Denmark."

The issue here is that most of us are terrified to look at who we are sexually. To our way of thinking, people are either gay or straight. How about posing this question: "What would my life look like if I were both heterosexual and homosexual? How would my happiness quotient skyrocket if sexual preference were not the be-all and end-all of who I am? And what if it were more natural to live as a man or a woman with the androgyny of consciousness as opposed to either one or the other?"'

Men and women these days are entering into "spiritual love" relationships without the sexual component. They seek a deep bond without the confusion and diminishing returns of sexual politics. We call this phenomenon agape love, or Zen love. Women especially have often found greater comfort, tenderness, caring, and safety with other women than they have experienced with their boyfriends or husbands.

As a case in point, Oprah recently said that she and close friend Gayle King are not gay; they are not lovers. Oprah explained, "There isn't a definition in our culture for this kind of bond between women. So I get why people have to label it—how can you be this close without being sexual?" Winfrey went on to add, "Something about this relationship feels otherworldly to me, like it was designed by a power and a hand greater than my own. Whatever this friendship is, it has been a very fun ride."

There are a lot of deep friendships between women and women and men and men who seem to be soul mates, not bed mates. Oprah has settled into a comfort zone of love without sex that so many people have begun to embrace.

If I knew Oprah, I would tell her to say to anyone who asked if she were gay: "Do you need for me to be?" That would throw the light of inquiry back on those who really would like to ask themselves that question, but can't or won't.

Gay couples have the same issues as do straight couples. Homosexual people, in their struggle to be who they are and love who they choose, seem to imitate straight behavior in relationships. Homosexual men and women adopt children, get married where it is legal, and stay together or break up just like heterosexual couples. But gay men and women are given grief about their sexuality, because straight people are terrified to deal with what they perceive to be such a dark part of themselves. In an effort not to deal with their latent homosexuality, straight males transfer their gay tendencies onto homosexuals. These repressed qualities come out when a supposed straight man calls a homosexual "faggot," "limp wrist," "sick homo," or other inappropriate names, or when he beats up, hazes, or even murders a man who is gay. Women tend to be more sympathetic and empathetic to gay men and women. But when the organized religion weighs in on homosexuality, gay men and women are condemned.

The hot-button issue of invisible partners is not sexual preference. Whether we're gay or straight or gay and straight makes no difference—these are illusions that hide true feelings. Until we integrate our shadow with ourselves, who we live with and love doesn't matter. We are going to have the same defective no-win partnership.

You are neither gay nor straight. You are both. You choose the sex partner who best satisfies your karma. Don't judge others for the choices they make.

Homosexuality dressed up as straight and married, in both men and women, has been alive and well throughout history. The closet door has only been blown open in the past thirty or forty years because those who have been playing the straight life want to be free of the lie. My position is that it is not either/or, we are both.

Men have more trouble accepting their femininity than do women the male within. Tell a woman that she's predominantly masculine in actions and mind-set, and she accepts it and is often flattered. A man immediately defends his masculinity and declares his heterosexuality. This is a manifestation of his insecurity and discomfort with his softer side.

The good old boys' network is a manifestation of repression of a man's anima—the inability to recognize and integrate the nature of the feminine within him—which led to fear that women would show men up in the boardroom. Men are now acknowledging that women can be as talented and as tough in business as men are and they should be paid equally. And women are proving that they are better at many things men have always considered their bailiwick.

We can integrate the parts of ourselves that engage in destructive behavior, such as spousal abuse, sexual abuse, gay bashing, and violence toward people of color, so that we can live and let live. The first step to integration, resolving the problem with the shadow, is to accept that it is part of us, to make friends with the shadow in order to heal.

For clarification, in my experience, homophobia is fear that you are gay, not repulsion of someone who is. If you don't deal with your repressed homosexuality, your relationships will be total projection with no satisfaction.

Because we are really androgynes, we cannot become who we really are until we balance our outward identity with our inner shadow selves. We are not capable of bonding with the man or woman of our dreams, because the nightmare of separation from self won't let us. The nightmare of separation is a state of being unable or unwilling to get professional help in dealing with that inner world where the shadow lives. Maiming and killing one's spouse, or stalking a lover who has spurned us or lashing out at an ex because he or she won't reconcile are deadly outcomes to those nightmares.

I have a forty-something-year practice dealing with people who have been confused about themselves. It is not what you bring to a relationship, gay or straight, that makes you whole and happy. It is what you allow you to give to you.

TRANSFERENCE OF YOUR SHADOW

I had a California client a few years ago who eventually divorced her husband because he wouldn't let their son Josh take ballet lessons. The father, a football coach, said, "No son of mine is going to put on a pair of tights and flit around on a stage for his family and friends to see. Little boys play sports; girls dance."

The son was allowing his softer side to express itself, but because his father had always undervalued and denied his own feminine side, he projected his homophobia onto his son.

Josh became a leading dancer in one of the country's finest ballet companies. I had lunch with Josh after he became a *premier danseur,* and he told me that his father—the all-man football coach who had shamed his son about ballet—had sexually molested him and his older brother from the age of five until they left for college at eighteen.

"Your father transferred his shadow to you, refused to deal with his dark side, and his shadow drove him to act out sexually with you," I told Josh.

A recurring theme in my counseling with men and women is sexual abuse by an adult when the client was four or five or six years old. The abuse often continued into adolescence and longer. Many women have been sexually violated by their fathers and brothers. It is epidemic the number of women who have been sexually abused by their fathers when they were children without anyone ever knowing about the incest. It only stopped when the young women went off to college. Boys have experienced the same inappropriate touching by adult men. Catholic priests are not the only men who have scarred young boys and girls.

The repression of our shadow can get us into a lot of trouble at the worst times. The shadow will rattle its cage. It says, "I want to be heard," and it will appear at the most inappropriate times. Once when I was drinking at a country club function in Mobile, Alabama, I said something salacious about my date, a Magnolia blossom from the Deep South. She fled from the room, and the town talked about my bad-boy behavior for years. My anima, or shadow, whom I call "Alexandra," got drunk and embarrassed me because I would not deal with her.

We need to see that what we don't like in our partner can benefit us if we claim the unattractive traits as our own, and deal with them. A weekly powwow with our partner can open the door to healing our breakdowns and their root causes. Play the blame game with your partner, and you will lose every hand. Change you and change the kind of relationships you attract.

When unintegrated, an invisible partner can create havoc and mayhem. Talk to a recovering drunk and see how many times he ended up in bed with a stranger. Ask him about his credit rating or career history. How many marriages? Our shadow drives us into these insane debaucheries. We cannot afford to marginalize the kind of power our invisible partner wields. It renders us pitifully and incomprehensibly demoralized.

Remember that poem by Robert Louis Stevenson that

you learned as a kid: "I have a little shadow that goes in and out with me . . ."? No matter how much we try to get someone else to live out our character defects by projecting them, they stick to us like chewing gum to a shoe. Or they boomerang back where they belong.

The concept of an invisible partner is new to most of us. If you don't face the fear of what this invisible partner business is all about, you'll live with bad marriages, sink under huge alimony payments, or end up raising kids alone as a single parent. These things will happen because you keep doing the same thing, expecting different results.

ACCEPTING YOUR SHADOW

So you're recognizing that you're the real culprit in your failed relationships. Good. But what's next? What can you do to change you to be able to have a good solid partnership with another person?

We can turn to Carl Jung for insights into how to find the authentic self—the one who can make us truly happy. He says that the only way to become the true self is to be individuated—to move away from herd mentality and the opinions of others and to make up our own minds about who we are and what we believe. Think for yourself. Do not be afraid to stand by what you know to be true for you.

Did you ever stop to think why a brilliant poet like Emily Dickinson would live in self-imposed exile? Have you a clue why spiritual teachers live in monasteries and geniuses like Nietzsche hide where we can't find them? They have been so individuated that they do not want to hear from those of us who are still immersed in the annoying fray, drawing attention to ourselves like the women of the nineteenth century who were so desperate to be noticed that they walked about with a monkey on a stick. They needed attention because they could not recognize their own intrinsic value.

Get honest with yourself, and stop rationalizing bad-boy, bad-girl behavior. Surrender to the notion that you'll never change anyone but yourself, then start to deal with your own issues and let others deal with theirs.

Since I was tall enough to get Miss Cooper's attention in the first grade, I have been asking tough questions. Suppose I ask you, "If your relationship isn't working, why do you stay in it?" Could your answer be "Because everybody else is in a relationship"? Or "Because it's expected of me"? Or how about, "Because I don't want to be alone"? These responses are not good enough and will only keep you sick and tired of the matches you make.

The paradoxes and the impossibilities of partnership are to be found in the golden aspects of the shadow. We all must unlearn a lot of behavior that has kept us mired in the defeat of failed partnering.

So how do you accept the shadow? How do you balance this dynamic that is an invisible but powerful part of you? And when you do, how will your life change?

1. Have a conversation with your shadow daily. And don't forget to name him or her. Ask questions and listen quietly for the answers.
2. Look at your sexuality with an open mind. Get in touch with your femininity if you are a man and your masculine side if you are a woman. Be courageous enough to face any latent homosexuality or bisexuality. A life history of all your sex partners will go a long way in sorting out patterns in why relationships have not worked for you. The American tragedy is that few of us have succeeded in finding inner peace and contentment, no matter what our sexual preference. Do some deep introspection about you and how you can be happy, joyous, and free being in a relationship with yourself.
3. Stop looking for Momma or Daddy in a relationship. Most people are unconsciously trying to find someone to take care of them or someone to care take of. They want the man/woman in their life to do what only their invisible partner can do.

4. Men, stop saying, "I can't do that—it's not manly." Women, accept that you can do most anything a man can do.

5. Communicate with your partner instead of talking at him or her. Communication should reflect a sensibility and consciousness that is androgynous, and not male- or female-slanted.

6. Stop people pleasing or caring what others think about how you live, think, or speak.

7. Do the deep-tissue-issue work by writing a life history, an inventory of all the troubling people and events that have misshaped your perception of you and your relationships. See in black and white where the stinking thinking started and let a trusted counselor help you remove these dark spots.

When you take these steps, the kind of man or woman you draw into your life will change. You will magnetically attract more balanced relationships. You'll get what you deserve. It's the law of attraction.

All you've got to do to free yourself from the trap of ego-based desires is to stop playing the game. Refuse to get into compulsive, obsessive death-spiral relationships. The next time someone asks you to hop in the sack for a night of fun, tell him or her that your insurance for careless sex quit paying off. Say no—hell, no.

The more you choose to clean and clear relationship

stinkos out of your life, the closer you'll get to self-esteem and self-worth. And, don't forget, the sooner you'll get home.

Accept the fact that nobody's going to make you happy but you. Look at the poor examples for love that you got from your parents. No matter how you disdain your mother for being a doormat or your dad for being a bully, you have the same issues, whether you know it or not. Your parents imprinted you, and you can't escape their rotten qualities until you rewire your thinking and redraw your blueprint.

Make it okay to be alone. Go to parties and even be willing to travel unescorted. If you define your life only through relationships, you'll draw the wrong one every time the partner cards are dealt.

Reconnect to a relationship with a power greater than yourself. God will put the perfect partner in your life when He is ready for you to have one. Or you may find that a relationship with yourself is all you need. The greatest fallacy is that everyone should be in a relationship or married. Some of us were born to be alone. Not everyone is supposed to or wants to be married. When I look out at the landscape of life and see all the misery in marriage, I wonder why so many do it.

Each of us is on a path to return home. God waits for us to make a choice to clear away all blocks, barriers, and impediments to remembering who we really are. Relationship difficulties are the major pitfall to clearing.

Within you is a consciousness that can speak to you, that can guide you toward the conscious and authentic man or woman you were meant to be. Get quiet. Be still. Listen for the still small voice of inspiration that will lead you to your clearing.

CHAPTER 7

Stage Six—Forgive and Forget-Me-Nots

Forgiveness is a tricky business.

As kids, when we fall out with a school chum, it doesn't take much for us to go hand in arm with a best buddy or girlfriend once more. We fight, holler, and accuse, pick up our marble and storm off—and then, in a moment, the feud is over and we act as if nothing ever happened. Yet it seems so much more difficult to forgive and to forget when we're adults.

UNDERSTANDING FORGIVENESS

Here is how I embraced the stage of forgive and forget. I asked a question of my higher consciousness.

"Paul, explain to me why as we get older, we seem to get mad faster and stay madder longer, sometimes for years. Why is forgiveness harder?"

Albert, until a child is two, he is still living in the perfect world consciousness that he was born with. Having come more recently from the Upper World—where there is only peace and harmony and souls are as One (the ego is not functional "there")—the tiny child is still connected to this resonance of bliss.

At three, the ego wheedles its way into that perfect world connection and begins, much as a tutor, to teach the child the rules of the egocentric game of life: It's not about playing fair and making amends. It's about winning at all cost.

I learned a lot from my High Self about where we make wrong turns and how these dangerous neighborhoods appear on our life path.

The ego opens its syllabus and begins to disconnect the little ones through contamination. It teaches them how to "get even," "fight to the death," "never say you're sorry," and that "it's a dog eat dog world." As we grow up the ego is with us every step of the way and we get more resilient and tougher and more determined to be right in a fight.

Remember Darwin's "survival of the fittest"? Man begins to see living in the world as scrapping in a jungle, and with the ego's help, man fights for his selfish rights and he never wants to admit that he is wrong.

When he is ready and receptive and the dark world of the ego has flattened him through all the ways it will— too much booze, drugs, illicit affairs, anger, rage, narcissism, greed, and many other dastardly means in its bag of trick—man surrenders and turns to his Higher Self. That Higher Self is his conduit back to the ways of the world over "there"—and how to reconcile with others who struggle to return home.

But Paul also showed me that the way to be happy again, to see others as my pilgrims trying to change their ways with a different syllabus and a different way back to peace and harmony, we must seek forgiveness from those we have harmed. But keep in mind that forgiveness is a two-way street. Both parties are engaged in the lessons to be learned through the process of admitting one is wrong. Recently I was talking to a friend over breakfast about someone else, and I disagreed firmly with an opinion my friend had about this third party. In stating my case, I overstepped boundaries of decorum by listing my breakfast companion's defects of character. A small emotional skirmish ensued. In the end, she made amends for speaking about our mutual friend as she had and I made amends for being curt with her. Both of us were at fault and both of us cleared the air with the other.

But none of us can fake how we feel toward those who have harmed us. Words and actions damage us and we cannot pretend we are not bothered. However, I have learned the hard way that telling someone that they have bruised us and owe us amends never works.

To be free of the bondage of self and others, we must heal resentments. I came to believe that I had to make a list of my enemies and express my anger and rage toward them on paper as a first step to forgiveness. I was warned by Paul that I must forgive myself first.

RAGE IS A STEP TO FORGIVENESS

Rage is a gargantuan part of forgiveness. You've got to express your rage before you can forgive. I suggest that you make two lists: one of all the people you have harmed and another of all the people who have harmed you. Write each person in the second group the nastiest, meanest letter you can conceive. Go deep into repressed rage pockets and come up with some real barn-burner potshots. Let 'em have it. No holds barred.

That's what I did, and it worked. I still use this exercise to heal relationships with those I find unforgivable. Don't mail the letter, and never lay someone low with angry confrontation. Talk these feelings over with a counselor, someone you trust.

People who have harmed you may or may not respond the way you'd want them to if they ever read your tirade about how you've been wronged by them. Don't expect them to say they're sorry. Their response doesn't matter—that's why you're not sending the letter. It's how you accept your feelings that counts, especially because you cannot control how other people act or react, but you can control what you do.

I will never forget Martin from Miami, Florida, who was one of the most rage-filled men I have ever worked with. When he came to Sedona to work with me and my support team he was in his early fifties and in a gay relationship. He had been married right out of college, but soon realized he was gay, and divorced.

His maternal grandmother had raised him because his beautiful, selfish, and narcissistic mother Barbara Jean was too busy getting married, divorced, and remarried to care about him and her other children. When she died she had been married seven times.

When Martin came out of the closet, Barbara Jean loathed him and she cut him out of her life and out of her will. Martin and his mother had no contact. When his grandmother was dying—the woman who in essence had been his real mother—Barbara Jean refused to let Martin see her. She hired security guards to keep him away from the funeral and memorial service.

Martin really hated his mother. When Barbara Jean died, she left her considerable fortune to his sister and a stepsister. Martin got one dollar.

When I asked him to write his mother a rage letter,

he pulled out all the stops and decimated her. In all my years, I had never read more gut-wrenching vile and nasty things written about a person than what Martin wrote in his letter to "Mommie Dearest."

But he refused to write her an amends letter. "I hate that bitch with all that is unholy. I will not forgive her."

But he did forgive her. The next day, a miracle happened. At his private letter-burning ceremony of forgiveness, having meditated and entreated Mother Father God to hear his letters of forgiveness, Martin got out his yellow pad and wrote his mother this letter:

Mother, I have unmercifully raged at you. I would never nominate you for Mother of the Year. Having said this, somewhere in time—in that place over "there" as Albert says, you have been able to see my struggle and you know that I must look at my part in the play we wrote each other into.

Mother, I have always wanted you to love me, to help me accept that I am a homosexual, but you never did. Your hatred for me because I was gay devastated me. Throughout my life I have wanted you to love me and care for me and accept me as I am.

Today I had an epiphany. I realized that in order for me to seek your forgiveness I needed to see the harm I have done to you. The program that I have been

attending here in Sedona says that there are always
two people involved in a fight. In order to clear away
the hurt feelings and make things better, I have to seek
forgiveness for my part in the bad blood.

As a first step to being able to seek your forgiveness,
I have forgiven myself for all the things I have done
to hurt you and others. I have been able to connect
to my true self and to see that I was under the pall of
deep and dark negative guidance from my ego—not
me—not who I am—as a way to get to forgiveness—as
a way to free myself from my dark side and from the
dark side of other people.

Mother, I ask you to forgive me for the mean and
vicious thoughts I have put out into the world about
you and toward you, and for the bad things I have
said about you. Albert says that words kill as much
as actions. I want to ask God to bless your life and
wherever you are I ask the Divine to love you and to
bless your soul.

Mother, I love you with all my heart.

Expressing your anger and rage is a precursor to being
able to get to the mother lode of love and forgiveness. But
as with Martin, all forgiveness is about forgiving yourself
first—no matter what the circumstances and no matter
who did what to whom.

OPRAH-ESQUE CONFESSIONS
AND MAKING AMENDS

When I was writing this chapter, A.J. Hammer of *Hollywood Insider* did a segment about Oprah Winfrey, who had recently confessed to having had an affair with a married man when she was in her twenties. Hammer's expert guest felt that Oprah's nature is to just let things flow, to say things in a kind of stream of consciousness—and never to offer excuses for her behavior. Oprah said that she had hurt another man's wife and expressed her disgust with herself for having done so. The expert guest concluded that, "Oprah is just being Oprah—honest and open about her past. No one ever need drop a rumor on the public about her because she has already done it."

I don't know whether or not Oprah Winfrey ever made direct amends to anyone, but I do know she benefited by copping a plea to her behavior.

I write about this because not only are amends necessary for forgiveness but it is confession that starts the process and makes the whole ordeal less shocking and dreadful. Once you have spoken about something you have done or something you've said to or about someone, even if it boomerangs back to you, the news has no power. You have defused it with open-faced confession. Let the chips fall where they may.

Forgiveness comes in waves of recognition at inevitable times in our lives when we need to stop the fight and angst with family and friends, or enemies, so we can enjoy the struggle to become who we were born to be.

An important stage of redevelopment of true self is making amends, and it starts with a list—the "A" list. The listing of those to whom I must come clean is necessary to let me be at peace with myself.

The first name on my list of people who did me the most harm was me. I had to face how I had been the father of all my shame, disappointments, and unfinished business with God—how He created me to be one person, and I was determined to be someone else. It was only with guidance from the ego that I got to fail at the life I thought I was supposed to live. The ego helped me destroy the false self with alcoholic behavior. This was how my dark side had colluded with my light, to help me find the real me under the rubble of my inauthentic self.

To realize that all misdeeds were mine but not committed by the authentic me brought me little solace. I liken karmic debts to a crime scene. Even though I knew the real me was blameless, that it was my ego leading me down the primrose path to wrong choices, my fingerprints were on all my misdeeds. If I could somehow, with astute guidance from a counselor or mentor, inventory my life and see where I went wrong, I could make amends to those I had harmed and ultimately forgive myself.

I dared not shortchange this process. I had to face all of my transgressions and ask forgiveness of myself and those I had harmed. Buried deeply and oftentimes for-gotten were shameful things that I had done or that oth-ers had done to me—which became secrets that I would not share under penalty of death. They had to be dredged up and exposed in order to heal.

Not all amends would be received with a kind and lov-ing "thank you and God bless you." Several years ago, I went to someone I had harmed to ask his forgiveness. He was the last person on Earth to whom I wanted to humble myself. When I was finished with my amends, he started in on me. This man told me that I was sneaky, irresponsible, and untrustworthy. He kept me in my seat for four hours—I was in his house—while he unloaded onto me every unrequited emotion he had about his wife and parents and all his friends and enemies. It was not easy, and I think I slept for twenty-four hours after tak-ing leave of his ranting. But I was free from him and my transgressions, because I got honest with myself and sought forgiveness from him.

An encounter with a banker was somewhat the same story. I gave an Oscar-worthy explanation—meek mixed with down-and-out in Sedona—about why I had not paid on my credit card. I threw in my bit about going to meet-ings and doing step work with my sponsor, and he re-sponded with a stone face, "If you're through with your cockamamie story, show me the money."

Other times, the response you get may be better than

you expected. I encountered a restaurateur whom I had stiffed for several thousand dollars. He was drinking too much the night that I ran into him, but when I approached him he asked me how I was.

I said to him, "Jerry, I owe you money, and I want to make financial amends."

"Albert, I know to the penny how much you owe my restaurant. You're sober—obviously I'm not—so take the money you owe me and help someone else trying to get sober. When someone needs something to eat, feed him. When a homeless man or woman stumbles into a meeting, give them shelter. Good luck to you. You came to me like a man, humbled yourself, and I respect that."

He turned and went back to his friends, but I have kept my end of the bargain through the years. Since that night I have repaid my debt as he asked me to do. It sounds saccharine to say, but Jerry was echoing scripture: "For I was hungry, and ye gave me meat: I was thirsty, and ye gave me drink: I was a stranger, and ye took me in. . . ."

The caterpillar wraps itself in a cocoon and emerges a butterfly. Your ego must go through a similar conversion. The ego must humble itself to God, die, and resurrect. The ego at one moment is the nefarious, deceitful, dishonest, dark part of you, and when you surrender and die to your false self, you are reborn a precious child of God. But you need to reaffirm your God-self daily because it often shape-shifts back to the ego self.

FORGIVING YOURSELF

Forgiving yourself is a prerequisite to forgiving others. God may be all-seeing and all-knowing, but He wants you to come to Him and admit your wrongdoing as a right step to freedom from the bondage of self and others. When you make amends, it makes your life cleaner, clearer, and better. To ask for forgiveness shows a desire to reclaim your birthright and be the legitimate you, who always was and always will be.

When you face the truth looking back at you from the karmic mirror, those who have harmed you are mere reflections of what you've done to hurt others. The more you forgive and ask for forgiveness, the closer you come to who you really are. Never say "I am sorry" or "I apologize." Rather say, "I want to make amends for what I have done to harm you." "I am sorry" and "I apologize" are passive-aggressive ploys that a lot of us use to get the heat off of us—and they are meaningless words—and don't clear the slate. To make amends means to change your behavior. Amends identify you as authentic and begin to separate you from the ego-driven self who harmed others.

Unless you make amends to those you have harmed, you will be tied to them forever. Your ex-husband will show up in every man you meet, because you never cleaned up the wreckage of your marriage. Refuse to ask your mother for forgiveness, and she will express herself in every new woman who comes into your life.

I am reminded of a client—a darling woman whom I'll call Sarah—who was rebellious, oftentimes without a cause, and she definitely walked to the beat of her own drummer.

When I met Sarah she was thirty-eight and divorcing her third husband. She was perky and precocious, and she believed that if she slept with a man, she should be married to him first.

We discovered in the review of her life history that each of her husbands was an alcoholic, a womanizer, and—interestingly—had been fired from jobs for mismanagement of company funds or, plainly put, embezzlement.

"Why would a girl like me marry the same kind of man three times? I'm not stupid!"

In opening her closet door we found a lot of incriminating evidence that she was doing the same thing expecting different results, which we in twelve-step meetings refer to as insanity.

Her father and stepfather were both attractive, alcoholic, womanizing men who had gone to jail for stealing company funds. Rather than taking a hard, cold look at their criminal behavior, Sarah thought her father and stepfather "were great men who happened to have drunk a little too much, whom women found irresistible, and who happened to have been caught filching a little money from the people they worked for." She had never seen the connection until we exposed the umbilical cord of her dysfunctional behavior.

Sarah eventually came to understand that because she had never been honest about the reprobate men who raised her, she had attracted the same kind of men into her adult life. When she finally Windexed the dark, dirty glass she'd been looking through, she saw the pattern and why.

To clean up her side of the street, she went to each ex-husband and made amends for expecting them to be loving and supportive and monogamous and honest. She confessed that she had been carrying around a magnet for drawing each of them to her. She needed to understand she had created each husband to fulfill her egocentric sick dependence on men who were not dependable, as she had done with her father and stepfather.

Forgiving herself and seeking forgiveness from the men allowed each of her ex-husbands an opportunity to make amends to her. And most of the time when you make amends to someone it opens the door of willingness for that person to ask forgiveness from you. Selfishness and self-seeking will fade and vanish. Remorse, self-pity, and feelings that no one loves you will melt under the light of love and forgiveness.

ACCEPTING AND EXPECTING AMENDS

Just because you make amends to someone, don't expect them to accept it. Making the amends is the freedom of the act. Remember the instance with my banker—he was not interested in why I had not paid the bank. Amends to him was settling up with the bank.

Oftentimes, we feel that others owe us amends. In all my experiences, such expectations set you up for major disappointment. If you think someone owes you amends, examine why you think they do. Don't forget that you are the common denominator in all the amends you need to make. Look at what you need to seek forgiveness for. If a person who stirs you with resentment never seeks forgiveness from you, make it okay. Clear away your part in the stinking thinking and high drama in which you star.

There are famous cases of bitter rivals becoming bosom buddies, like Elizabeth Taylor and Debbie Reynolds. Liz stole Debbie's husband Eddie Fisher in the 1960s, yet the two of them kissed, made up, and starred a few years ago in a Movie of the Week. Bill Clinton beat George H.W. Bush for President in 1994, yet in 2005 they toured tsunami-hit South and Southeast Asia and set aside their political differences to raise a lot of money worldwide to restore these countries. (Maybe they're not bosom buddies, but they could do good work together.)

What should we do when we're frustrated and angry with a person who doesn't ask for forgiveness, but we want them to? Pray for them. I was told to pray for someone for thirty days and the resentment and anger would be gone. Try it. It works.

FORGET-ME-NOTS

The most powerful promise of making amends is that old saw, "What doesn't kill you makes you stronger." And Ernest Hemmingway weighed in with, ". . . stronger in the broken places." Amends have a way of making us better and it is because we are broken down and separated from the anger and resentments we have felt in the past for others.

We say in recovery circles, "We will not regret the past nor wish to shut the door on it," which is my way of talking about forget-me-nots. Those whom I have perceived as my most feral enemies end up becoming my greatest teachers.

There was a boy named Kenny in my tenth grade French class who said something hurtful to me one morning and I never forgot his words. For years everything that I did was prismed through those three biting words. As we were translating a passage about St. Francis, the teacher asked if any of us knew where Assisi was. Kenny hollered, "There's a sissy," and pointed at me.

Kenny's outburst helped me understand eventually that he was seeing my feminine side, which would one day be the golden part of my humanity. It was first brought to my attention by what seemed like, at the time, an infantile comment. He was an archeologist for me: "I have stirred you up. I have led you to buried treasure, so start digging." He was not shaming me, rather, he was helping me to uncover the bedrock of the work I would do most of my adult life: integration of the male and female within each of us. What appears to be one thing, with time and wisdom, turns out to be something entirely different.

In *On Death and Dying*, author Elisabeth Kübler-Ross referred to difficulties in life as windstorms—slights by friends, alienation from our children, getting fired from a job, and even divorce from the one with whom we said, "til death doth us part"—which eventually turn out to be touchstones. I call them forget-me-nots.

CHAPTER 8

Stage Seven—Bringing Your Brother to the Light

Helping someone see the light—to change dramatically, to see the errors of his behavior—is one of the strongest admonitions of Kabbalah: "Receive the light to share." And in this instance sharing the light simply means to shepherd your friend, your brother or sister back into God's fold.

As all are both dark and light and all are created by and of God, when one returns to God, he must bring with him others who need to be transformed. It is not enough to surrender to the error of one's former actions and deeds in this and past lives. You must be willing to lead others back to God.

But there are more basic survival needs that people all around us have—the need for food and shelter and protection from abuse and man's inhumanity to man. It is one thing to need a spiritual renaissance, but first things first. Feed the poor and heal the sick.

In the spirit of interconnectedness and interrelatedness we must be watchful of those around us who need our help. I am not a bible thumper, but I draw from the incredible lessons to be learned from this powerful document of God's will for our lives.

To support the call to "receive the light to share," the King James Version of the Bible says in Matthew 25:

For I was hungry, and ye gave me meat: I was thirsty, and ye gave me drink: I was a stranger, and ye took me in.

Naked, and ye clothed me: I was sick, and ye visited me: I was in prison, and ye came unto me.

Then shall the righteous answer unto him, saying, Lord, when saw we thee hungry, and fed thee? or thirsty, and gave thee drink?

When saw we thee a stranger and took thee in? Or naked, and clothed thee?

Or when saw we thee sick, or in prison, and came unto thee?

And the King shall answer and say unto them, Verily I say unto you, inasmuch as ye have done it unto one of the least of these my brethren, ye have done it unto me.

I don't know about you, but when I hear parables— whether written by Paolo Coelho or someone else in modern times or by Zohar, the oldest written religious authority known to man—I am touched. I get a chill down my spine and I am moved to action.

This parable reminds me that I am responsible when I see or hear of a need and if I can meet that need then I must.

Within all is the light. The light may dim, and you may feel that God is dead. It is not true. As long as some- one is there to lead the way, the lost one may return to the path.

A longtime friend, Joseph Braswell, called a couple of years ago to tell me that he loved me. Joseph had been diagnosed with pancreatic cancer that winter and chose not to go through chemotherapy. The voice within told me to write Joseph a note every week, which I did, and to make brief phone calls to him.

When we talked we spoke about the great adventure that lay ahead of him and how the soul continues when the body dies. He thanked me for not patronizing him by talking about a miracle cure, but rather for support- ing his decision to move forward rather than go to any lengths to prolong his life. Oftentimes we laughed out loud about some of the silly things we had done and also about how seriously he had always taken himself.

Joseph told me one night that we were soul brothers,

because he cared for me as much as I cared for him, and that we had helped one another along the spiritual path. We were each other's keeper.

When Joseph died, he was looking ahead, not behind him. He is now enjoying his great adventure called life after life.

Continue to still your mind. Go always deep within yourself, where God is. Slow down. Look back and see who falters and falls when his heart wants to go home. Reach out and pull the one who stumbles nearer to you.

See God in everyone. Bring your brother to the light.

MEETING VICTOR

In 1989, I focused on spiritual lessons in meditation, and truth walked in just as Paul had that first afternoon. Like one trying to become accomplished at the piano, I practiced what I had been given: I prayed with diligence and I listened for God's answers. Making notes in a journal daily speeded up the process of my clarity by allowing me to see when my ego was trying to creep back into my life. Most of all, I became aware of what I could do for others—to get out of myself.

The clearer I became, the more I accepted who I was, and the fewer expectations I had of myself and others. I woke most days waiting for what God wanted me to have and to do.

Little did I know that I was about to meet someone who would test me and my capacity to give to someone else what I had found to be of benefit to me. The underpinning of the new me was to give away what I had been given.

One day I made plans to meet a friend at a restaurant in Sedona. I was on a low-fat diet, and this restaurant offered spectacular desserts made with fudge, peanut butter, and butterscotch filling. I spied a fruit tart that fit my diet, so I bought it.

As I sat down, a man at another table asked "Let me know if you like that fruit tart."

I took a bite and said, "No fat, not fried, no sugar . . . no taste. Try it. Not bad."

Two couples sat opposite me and my friend. One of four was the man who had asked me about the tart. He was of average height, blond haired, with piercing hazel eyes.

Our eyes locked. There was a moment of recognition.

"I saw your picture in the paper today," I said to him.

"What paper?" he asked.

"*USA Today*," I replied.

"What was I doing?" he wanted to know.

"You were jogging with the president of the United States," I responded.

"I'm amazed that you recognized me. I was running with the president and ten other S.E.A.L.s with my head down. How did you spot me?" he asked.

I shrugged with an "I don't know" look on my face.

"I'm Victor Meyer." He introduced his wife and brother, and their friend.

We all shook hands. My friend introduced himself and then said, "Don't ever ask how Albert knows anything. Knowing what the rest of us don't is his business."

I had to leave for a personal training session in ten minutes. Victor apparently worked out a lot. He was robust, tanned, and very healthy looking. I had the feeling I "knew" him.

Before I left, I told him to visit the Los Abrigados Sedona Health Spa, and that I'd have passes left for him at the desk.

On Monday when I returned to the spa, I found that Victor had left his name and address for me. I sent him a letter describing why he seemed intuitively familiar to me. Victor sent me a French picture postcard of a child with the words *Tu es mon ami,* you are my friend. Our notes crossed in the mail. I have always felt that I lived in France around the time of the French Revolution. I am very drawn to the Napoleonic period, and years ago I hung a large John Dawson oil painting of Napoleon in my living room.

Several months later, I got a telephone call from Victor. He would be driving through Sedona in a few days and wanted to know if he could stop by. The French Navy had accepted him into its two-year exchange S.E.A.L.

program. He would be stationed near Marseilles in the south of France.

At 5:30 on a Sunday afternoon, the doorbell rang. I opened the door and there stood Victor.

"Come in," I said cordially, shaking his hand and helping with his garment bag.

He looked at me with those intense eyes and said quizzically, "What am I doing here, and why do you have a portrait painting of Napoleon on that wall?"

Victor's question precipitated hours of discussion about reincarnation, why certain people are brought back together, and what the reunion is all about. "You pick right back up where you left off," I said. "Sometimes it's just to say 'Hello, good-bye,' and at other times you have to complete unfinished business."

We joked for awhile about which one of us had been Napoleon. Truth be told, he and I were together in that historical period. I also got intuitive flashes that we had been in the Vatican together and in the dynasty of Ramses II in Egypt.

He said that he had been raised a Baptist, and that Baptists don't believe in reincarnation. "Unfortunately, I, too, was a Baptist until I left divinity school at nineteen. Thank God I found booze instead of the ministry," I said, watching for his reaction.

Later at dinner, Victor asked how I knew we had been together in a past life.

"I just know it. My intuition tells me that we synchronistically met that morning because we have unfinished business. We made a date telepathically to be there on the same day and at the same time. The minute I saw you, felt your energy, I knew that I knew you. When you spoke, the sound of your voice confirmed it," I said.

"Some of your ideas are strange, Albert, but I am very attracted to what you have to say, for a couple of reasons. First, you're so positive and energetic with how you say things. And secondly, I do feel this powerful energy exchange. How do you know it's a past-life connection?" Victor asked.

"I don't know. You just have to trust your gut instinct. Intuition is the wavelength of recognition. Give it time. Soon you will know if our reunion is going to be for mutual benefit or if we have unpleasant karmic situations to work through," I said.

Over dessert, Victor said, "This is interesting, but how could Christians and Catholics have been so wrong about reincarnation? They flatly deny it exists." He was not telling me anything I didn't know. My preacher back home told my family that astrology and reincarnation were concepts of "the devil." Today, Catholics are beginning to have access to documents supporting both astrology and reincarnation that have been sealed in vaults in the Vatican for centuries.

"You forgot the Jews," I said. "The Kabbalah and the

Zohar teach that all of us reincarnate to refine the soul. The church, like the state, doesn't want to lose control over its members (or constituencies), so it disavows any information that doesn't affirm what it wants us to believe. It's about control rather than what is true. Jewish mysticism says that not only must you live life after life, but that your astrology birth chart is the roadmap for your life. Your birth chart points out your positive qualities and negative traits, what you need to atone for, what opportunities exist for you, and when these growth challenges will appear in your life.

"A lot of information has come to light in the last fifty years—the Dead Sea scrolls, the Nag Hammadi library, and the Gospel of Judas among them—to expose the lies of Christianity, and I mean all churches . . . Baptist, Episcopal, Unity, the Catholic Church, and many other sects. When the planet Pluto goes into Capricorn in 2008, there is a strong possibility that chaos will arise within organized religions," I said.

"I'm very drawn to everything you say, but I was raised to believe another way. Your points of view are strange on the one hand, but very appealing to me on another," Victor said.

"As a young boy, I was taught a lot of things that never made sense. I went to church. I sang songs. I was baptized. I loved the music, but the sermons never clicked with me. No matter how loud the preacher preached, no matter what he said, my still, small voice of intuition whispered, 'It's not true.' It would say, 'Keep looking.'"

"Albert, you are so darned passionate about things. Where does all this enthusiasm come from?" Victor asked.

"Pain and suffering. I tried to be someone I wasn't, and it nearly killed me. I took a death-spiral to rock bottom through booze and bad credit. I had to get out of where I was, no matter what price I had to pay. I have learned how to live by never wanting to live the way I lived before. I have found a God of my own understanding, not a bushel of bastardized Bible-thumping guilt trips. When I had played out the scene of running, hiding, and living in shame, I cleaned up the wreckage of my past and let God run the show. I made amends and never looked back."

It was time for a lighter note. Victor struck one with his innocence and candor. "Don't you find it interesting that I am a Baptist United States Navy S.E.A.L. search-and-destroyer, and you are a fallen Baptist who doesn't believe in war? How did we ever find each other, and what are we supposed to do now that we are back together?" he wanted to know.

I nodded and shrugged but remained silent.

"I have two years in France. I'll remain open to all of this new information. Send me all the metaphysical books you want me to read. I'll use your meditation tapes and keep a journal. As a matter of fact, why don't you come to Paris for Thanksgiving?" Victor asked.

"I'll come, but I pick the hotel. I have a suspicion that the government still believes you can see Paris on five dollars a day."

As we were paying the bill, Victor pulled at my arm and said, "You want to hear a strange coincidence? Your telephone number was my military number at the United States Naval Academy."

I am accustomed to synchronicities, gut reactions, click connections, intuitions, and miraculous signs, but it still takes me by surprise when one comes along. That's the kid in me. I never want to get so big for my britches that I don't get a thrill when I see one of God's flash cards.

I recognized Victor from a picture in the newspaper. What are the odds? We both have a passion for France— her cuisine and museums, her people and her history: the French Revolution, as well as Napoleon. His military number being the same as my telephone number cinched it for me. Meeting Victor Meyer was a God shot.

VICTOR'S TRANSFORMATION

I took a four-day holiday to Paris to see Victor, just as we had planned. Victor reported he had planned a full schedule for us. I was impressed at how much thought he had given to our Thanksgiving holiday.

"Tomorrow I thought we would go to Versailles, if you would like to see the grand palace of Louis XIV," Victor said.

"I'd love to see Versailles. Where do we go after that, my Francophile?"

"I know you like art. Tomorrow afternoon we'll go to the Barnes Collection at the Musée D'Orsay. The next day we'll take in the Louvre."

We left the hotel to explore. It was cold and damp, typical Paris weather for late November. Although Victor and I were new friends, our conversations were what you would expect from lifelong pals. He would speak and I would finish his sentence. I would say something and he'd say he was thinking the same thing at the same time. We were in sync.

Across the street from a café where we planned to eat dinner was a church.

"What church is that, Victor, do you know?"

"It is St-Germain-des-Prés. The church has a very interesting history. I'm reading about Comte Saint Germain in one of those books you sent from the Golden Word Bookstore in Sedona," he said proudly.

It is believed that Saint Germain was born in 1561. Legend has it that he was a master alchemist and was able to make himself invisible. He was known as "the man who never dies and knows everything."

St. Germain-des-Prés is the oldest church in Paris. It

was built by the Merovingian King Childebert in 542 to house holy relics. It was rebuilt during the eleventh century, and the nineteenth century, and again in the 1990s. From its inception, it was a very influential Benedictine abbey. During the French Revolution, it burned.

We ran across the street and into its dark and Gothic interior. A host of angels appeared to hover and float near the ceiling. My imagination ran amok. There was no question that something was astir here. I have a well-honed intuition as well as a vivid imagination. It must be the smoke cloud from all these candles burning, I thought, as my mind tried to reassure me.

There were the usual icons and relics. Candles blazed from wall sconces, and chanting echoed around the church. Congregants filled the chairs in the middle of the church and the benches near the altar.

We have a Catholic church in Sedona, the Chapel of the Holy Cross. Similar to St. Germain-des-Prés, people are encouraged to make a donation and light candles for the welfare of themselves and others. The practice was prevalent here, as worshipers lit candles and prayed.

Victor and I went to different parts of the church. I was drawn to the altar. Winter-bright flowers cascaded over the entry at the front of the cathedral. Rose-scented candles burned in heavy matte-green gold candelabra. I sat down on the front pew and fell into a swoon I know so well.

I heard nothing but the thunder of silence. Paul spoke to me.

Brother's Keeper Albert, you have been climbing Jacob's ladder. You are at a stage of your journey, remembering the lesson that you must bring your brother with you when you seek truth that leads to your redemption. But this example suggests that you come back with a brother or sister. You have selected Victor, an old friend from many lifetimes, to make the journey with you.

You two have met again so that he can be opened from within himself and access his storehouse of memories and Gnostic truths. He speaks about a lot of things that are not his ideas or his beliefs. Victor will trust the process as he begins to embrace his authentic self. He will change in his time. Do not judge a book by its cover. Watch how he transforms. Continue to use fairy tales and star power to help him as he unfolds. Ali Baba said to the cave, "Open, sesame," and it did. It will be the same with Victor. You have come back to give him his code.

"Paul, what should we do to help all the others who suffer from injustices and who are hungry and naked? What about men and women and children who speak a different language, worship in a mosque, and whose lives my government is destroying? Do I raise my voice against these atrocities? Do I vote my conscience of care and concern? Do I dare risk losing my comfort zone for the sake of being my brother's keeper halfway around the world, or next door?"

You are doing what you resonate to do. You reach out when you see a need. All of you are in this drama of transformation together, even those who have not awakened to the challenge.

BROTHER'S KEEPER

Has someone who needs your help crossed your path? Did you leave it to someone else to lend a helping hand, or did you offer your support or your resources? Would you be open to helping a young boy with a handicap from which he will never recover? Are you open to the still, small voice of God when He asks you to be your brother's keeper?

The Lord asks, "Where is your brother?" In our world of abject materialism, who will feed and clothe your brother if you don't? When you see the homeless, do you look the other way? Do you think that street people have brought their condition on themselves?

Kay Warren, wife of Rick Warren, who wrote *The Purpose-Driven Life,* is executive director of the HIV/ AIDS initiative at Saddleback Church in Lake Forest, California. She wrote an e-commentary for CNN, entitled "Christians must do more to combat AIDS, comfort victims."

She recorded an account of an African woman named Joana, emaciated with AIDS, who greeted her when Kay toured Mozambique. Joana had unrelenting diarrhea, little food, no earthly possessions, and only an elderly aunt who had taken pity on her to care for her needs. A short time later Joana died—rejected, abandoned, persecuted, and destitute. Warren writes, "I had no medication that could cure Joana, nothing to alleviate her pain, nothing that would restore her to health. But I offered her the one thing that all of us can offer: I offered my presence. I put my arms gently around her, prayed for relief from her suffering, and whispered, 'I love you.'"

This is the lesson of "brother's keeper" in practice. Another profound example is Captain Scott Southworth, who was serving in the U.S. Army in Iraq in 2003 when a three-year-old boy with cerebral palsy named Allah crawled toward him across the floor of the orphanage where Scott was volunteering. When Scott returned to the United States, he could not get Allah out of his mind. Something inside him spoke to Scott about wanting to take care of this boy, to be his father. Against the greatest odds, and with the cooperation of the U.S. Embassy in Iraq, Scott, who was not married, adopted Allah.

Brother's Keeper. This is the stage at which I want to be able to reach out and give assistance to anyone anywhere who needs my help. This is the Golden Rule, and this is what Christ and Buddha and Krishna taught us about how to treat others.

Are we our brother's keeper? Yes we are, and it is time

that we realize that our brother may be next door, but he is also thousands of miles away. Apathy perpetuates starvation, and it allows wars to continue to be waged.

OUR SOUL JOURNEY

I was Victor's Keeper.

Victor and I had been together many times. When he came back into my life, I felt no doubt that I had to help him remember his truth rather than stay blocked by dogma. He was searching for answers. I would help him find them where the questions were, within him.

Victor was a trained killer and I was a pacifist; I had never handled a gun—I favored gun control. He was a traditional Christian, and I was a man of many faiths. He stood ready to carry out the orders of the military, and I stood ready to dismantle his military orders to invade and harm civilians in a country that is not ours to occupy.

Paul asked:

Where is your brother, Albert? Are you your brother's keeper even if he does not share your beliefs? Can you "love thy neighbor as thyself?" Can you lead by example and let what you do speak louder than what you say? Can you love someone who is not lovable? Can you practice patience and nonjudgment to help your brother—the one God drew to you with the magnetism of compassion and concern?

When we met, the resonance of Victor's voice drew me to him. I heard him before I saw him. The moment he heard me speak, he listened and he was affected. Although our beliefs were different, our memory books of shared lives canceled out the differences. He learned from me and I from him. Difficulties would only arise when our wills would clash and our egos would deceive. I had to stay the course. I felt that my commission was to bring him to the light.

In past lives, he had been my student, my son, a friend, a brother. France is a karmic place for him and me. We both lived our last incarnation here, and it was here that we had to return to reactivate why we reunited.

I looked up and saw a painting of Saint Francis of Assisi. He was traveling by foot with his brother, a companion and fellow seeker. These men were committed to one another through God. Saint Francis required brothers to go out in twos, because the road was less lonely and the work less tedious. Companionship—brotherhood—is crucial to man's successful return to God.

Victor, like me, had assumed a false identity through his karmic bloodline. He was carrying historical memory of a father's and grandfather's transgressions. Victor would clear these issues and become who he really was as I let him know how I freed myself of family karma. This was as it had to be: when someone has a need for help which we can give, it is our assignment to give it.

I felt a nudge on my shoulder, and I opened my eyes and looked into an overpowering light which was radiating behind Victor.

"Albert, the church is about to close. I wondered where you were. I saw smoky haze and blinding light at the front of the cathedral. Are you all right?"

"I'm fine. I nodded off and it was difficult to come back from where I was. Victor, you have been nibbling around for an answer to why we met. Would it satisfy you to know that we are brothers?" I said as we exited the church.

"Albert, if we are brothers, I'd love to know who our mother is. She must be a hundred and one years old," he exclaimed as he ran to hail a cab, laughing at the prospect of Brother Albert, Brother Victor.

We went to Versailles the next day, saw a lot of art, and ate delicious food in small restaurants. It rained every day. We trudged through puddles and drank espresso and ate croissants all over Paris. It was the best four days I can remember.

"When you say that you are your brother's keeper, Albert, what exactly does that mean?" Victor asked.

"I talk a lot about the Holy Grail, as do you, Victor. To understand what the grail is we must answer the question, "Who am I?" We have to find out what is the purpose of our life. Trevor Ravenscroft writes in *Cup of Destiny* that you cannot come to the Grail unless you bring your brother. The Bible reminds us that we are our brother's keeper. Since all of us have fallen from grace, we must come back to God and bring someone who has also fallen from grace, our brother or sister. Coming back alone is receiving redemption for the self alone. We have to share redemption to receive it," I said.

When I had to leave, I told Victor, "I have loved everything about this vacation. It was meant to be. Seeing Paris with you had purpose."

Something inside me said that Victor and I would have more to talk about and would reconnect. Paris had been a new beginning. No matter how many times someone like Victor walks back into my life, it amazes me.

The next night, as I turned back the covers to get into bed, I found a package and a note on my pillow. And by the light of the tiny bedside lamp I read the note first:

Dear Albert,

I thank you for your love, your kindness, and your forthrightness. I'm having the time of my life. You are a teacher, a father, a friend, a brother.

Love,

Victor

I opened the package, and inside was a black hooded sweatshirt. A note pinned to it said:

This is one of the sweatshirts I had made for students in my S.E.A.L. training class last month. I felt like giving you one. Wear it with pride.
Victor

I unfolded the sweatshirt and on the back was stenciled "My Brother's Keeper." This was yet another eerie but confirming sign that there are no accidents. Victor and I had reunited for a powerful purpose.

I am my brother's keeper, and he is mine.

CHAPTER 9

Stage Eight—The Love Chapter: All You Need Is Love

You're reading about these stages, these lessons, because there's something in your life that you want to improve and nothing seems to be on more wish lists than loving and being loved. I suggest at first that you separate out agape or Zen love from boyfriend/girlfriend, boyfriend/boyfriend, girlfriend/girlfriend love, sexual explosions, and other fantasies. The need to be fulfilled as a spiritual being having the proverbial human experience is what most of us seek most.

In her bestselling book, *Eat, Pray, Love,* Elizabeth Gilbert reveals how insane one's life can get while going through a divorce from an unreasonable husband. In this travelogue of personal discovery she plucks out past patterns of toxic sexual love and replaces them with self-love. That love is found in God through day-after-day-after-day meditation. Gilbert apparently found true love and happiness after God knocked her for a loop to become primary in her life.

I didn't create these stages in a book, or contrive them to fit into neat little chapters so I could become your teacher. These stages became a part of my life, my personal growth, my journey, and I'm compelled to show others how they too can find what I have found. My life experiences have culminated into this moment, the eighth and final stage, where I am at a point of peace and sheer happiness.

I am feeling on top of the world. For once in my life, I am clean inside. Everything and everywhere I go, what comes to me is love, love, love. Man, I experience so many different kinds of love: courtly love, erotic love, familial love, free love, platonic love, puppy love, religious love, romantic love, unrequited love.

Then there is the love of God.

I had always wondered what I was living for and what my purpose was. What was revealed to me is that love is all there is.

It seemed that most of us had been trying to figure things out and reaching faulty conclusions. Let things be revealed, my voice of intuition whispered. The more I moved away from the consciousness of worldly desire, the more I experienced my connection with God. I felt better knowing who I was, and being driven by purpose rather than blind ambition. I heard over and over: "All there is, is love," and "Love is all there is." These phrases played in my mind like Bach, with words by Krishnamurti.

All there is, is love.

One voice with the perfect harmonics can change the world. You can make a difference if you speak from the clear and uncontaminated place of God.

THE SEARCH FOR LOVE

What have I learned about myself and love? When I am open and receptive to whom and what God puts in my life, the nature of love is effortless. If I continue to clear away what separates me from love, love finds me. I am so peaceful and euphoric in the presence of love's essence. I am so full of gratitude tonight. Love is all around me if I can open myself to it.

In Buddhism, according to Thich Nhat Hanh, a Vietnamese Zen Buddhist monk who was nominated by Martin Luther King for the Nobel Peace Prize, there are four elements of true love. (He describes them in his book *True Love*.) The first is loving-kindness or benevolence.

The second is compassion. Compassion is not only the desire to ease the pain of another person, but the ability to do it. The third element of true love is joy. Hanh says that without joy there can be no true love. And the fourth is freedom. When you love, you bring freedom to the person you love.

When I was a little boy, I yearned for someone to love me who knew me. When I was a little boy, I wanted someone who knew me to connect with me. And when I was a little boy, I wanted someone who connected with me to show me, not tell me about, love.

I did not feel loved by my family, nor was I able to love them. Later I learned that they did not have love to give, nor did I. The church's version of God's love did not click with me, either. Too many strings were attached to the love of God as the church laid it out.

I survived on self-righteous indignation in my down-the-rabbit-hole asylum. Inside myself, I talked to an invisible friend and listened to the music in my head. Going to school and trying to get along with family and friends were like personal appearances by "the entertainer" and "the pleaser." They were my false selves.

When I was a teenager, my minister's wife, Margaret Bowles, loved me as God would one day love me, but I could not accept her pure love. I was not ready to love and be loved.

Some cockamamie notion about lover relationships

settled into my subconscious with a thud and grew like ragweed. The light that penetrated my rat hole of shame told me that there were too many fish hooks in romantic love. The kind of love I craved was to be held, coddled, and cuddled, without having to prove myself lovable— or to be who others needed for me to be—in order to receive their love.

As I aged, pulp fiction and B movies took away the innocence of intuitively connecting with someone I just "knew" I was meant to meet and love. Fatuous haute couture models and studly celluloid boys so distorted what any of us could expect; thank God I found booze instead of trying to use these apparitions or illusions as roles for me to cast myself into.

As I got older, my cad of an ego goaded me to investigate the family fortunes of a couple of girlfriends to see if there was enough lucre to put me in the lap of luxury. I needed to validate my false social pretenses. My best-laid plan backfired. On a whim and in less than six weeks from the day we met, I married a dead-broke heiress who needed someone to support her. This was the time of my life when I was either boozing nightly or nursing a hangover. It was time for me to grow up and take responsibility for a wife. So what did I do to face the music like a man? I ran away.

FINDING LOVE

Love came to me through insanity in a no-exit play I wrote myself into. Booze was an elixir and comfort that emboldened me to rip and tear at everything and everybody when my craziness got too much for me to tolerate. I found a lot of wild and nutty people who would drive drunk with me with no headlights on and who lived life with no roadmap and no God.

Love came to me one dark and dreary night when, going the wrong way on a one-way street, the cops pulled me over and took me to jail. Sitting in that cell, I knew that I would either die or stop drinking and learn how to live booze-free—with honesty and integrity. The minute I surrendered and admitted that I was in a sanitarium with no locks and a prison with no guards, God walked into my life, abiding with me through prayer and meditation. I found that God loved me and connected with me. He really, really did love me and care for me. This was an open door to the freedom to love me and to love someone else.

When I was getting sober and recovering from "poor-little-ole-me-itis," my sponsor Bob told me to do for someone else what I would have liked someone to have done for me. "Albert, if no one ever took you by the hand and showed you the ropes of life, get over it by taking someone else by the hand and helping him find his place in the sun—the life God has for him if he can stop drinking and drugging."

Enter Scott.

When I met Scott he was waiting tables, and he did not look anything like the one I would take by the hand and help learn life's lessons. He was snarly and beefed-up with a Fu Manchu moustache. But the still, small voice said, "That's him." And I reflected back to the predictions by psychics that I had received many years earlier: *When you are around sixty years old, you will meet someone who has been your son in a former life; help him.*

I befriended Scott, brought him into recovery, became his sponsor, and all these years later, he and I are business partners. He says all the time that he would never have traveled the world and encountered the interesting people and cultures that he has, had he not gotten sober.

Scott has been the true joy of my life. What has caused our friendship to thrive is that we tell each other exactly how we feel, and we never lie about anything. We disagree but we stay with a problem until it is resolved. Scott is his own person, and I am, too. Love after sobriety has been different than my stabs at giving and receiving love when I was a drunk.

My client relationships have thrived, too, because they are born out of honesty. I am who my clients need for me to be. They use me as a mirror to see themselves. I had no idea that I would not only heal but would fall into the essence of twenty-four-carat-gold love while leading

189

clients to find their authentic selves. That is the miracle of what I do. My clients are my loves, and in spite of the rough row I make them hoe, I thrive when I am working. Second only to God, work is my love and my life.

I lay still in an open field and stretched out my arms.

I had come to realize that there were two worlds—the world of illusion and the world of reality. One was filled with fear and false creations of a divided self ruled by the ego. The other promised that all there is, is love. I am now at the good part of the play, and I love it.

In 1984 I got a phone call in Sedona from a woman in New York who said she heard someone talking about her astrology session with me at a cocktail party and wanted to book a session. I told her I would be in New York in two weeks, so she booked an appointment. She later told me that I had her at "hello" because she always got a yes or no about somebody from their voice.

Mrs. Arthur Hornblow, Jr., whom I knew as Leonora but café society called "Bubbles," taught me more about love in twenty-two years than I had ever learned from anyone else. The moment she walked into my life, I knew that I was the cosmic *consigliere,* but she was in charge of everything else. Leonora was tough, and she could be profane. When someone hurt me or caused me to withdraw because of their harsh words or actions, she was all over the detractor's case. She would say things like, "You are the best person who ever lived on this planet, and I know because I know most anybody who is worth knowing and you are tops. Get them out of your life. Rescind the association by chanting, 'Evil spirit return to your keeper.'"

When Leonora disapproved of something I intended to do, she would say to me, "Darling, that's the dumbest thing I've ever heard. If you do such an idiotic thing, never call me again." But she loved me by her actions, and when my soul was sore she provided balm.

Mrs. Hornblow was the leading lady God chose to coddle me and cuddle me—to spoil me rotten—and to see the best in me. If I know what love is, she gave me the vocabulary.

The Bells—the family I always wanted—are true friends who have come into my life with unconditional love. David Bell knows how to make me laugh, and he loves me when I cannot love myself. His wife Gail is a brilliant actress, very beautiful, but more important, very giving and loving. When she calls me up, she always wants to know, "What can I do for you?"

The children—Ashley and Andrew—stir my envy when I realize how much more special they are than I have ever been. The Bells were able to bring a love of family back into my life. There is greater honesty in communication with the Bells than there was in my biological family. We laugh ourselves silly at everything. Andrew and I keep up with tennis matches as if they were the most important things in the world. Andrew, who was born intuitive, and I help one another realize that tennis is only a game and any player on any given day can win whether we like him or her or not. We definitely have our favorites, and when someone we don't like wins, we can act like two-year-olds—but most of the time we are okay with who comes out on top. Ashley, who has the finest operatic soprano voice I have ever heard, the Metropolitan Opera and La Scala notwithstanding, vocalizes all day long, which raises the vibration in the house and in our hearts. She is precious to me for I see God in her and He speaks through her when she sings. The love I feel toward them and from The Bells must be what God intended, because He laughs out loud with us.

LOVE LETTERS

From childhood, I believed that nobody loved me, that something was wrong with me. I got these false impressions from my parents, who were unable to instill in me a sense of being worthy of their love. I have lived long enough to remember why I had chosen my family, what amends I had to make for past transgressions, and what was my destiny. Angels awaited my willingness to let go of the world of illusion and embrace the light of the world God created. Awareness of the real world was not enough to let me act in accordance with divine principle. First I had to become aware of the rules in returning to God's world and let go of false doctrines, mores, and customs of the ego world.

Love has its requirements. If you hurt someone, quickly amend that injury with humble admission. Glamour girls may be appeased by flowers and oversized bling, but true love springs from the way we nurture one another. If you care for someone in the name of love, show it by how you treat her, rather than with materialism. I am astounded by the number of people who measure love by what money can buy.

If you love someone, write him a love letter. Start by making amends for anything stupid or thoughtless you have done, to clear the air. Love blossoms with kind and considerate amendments to the way a relationship has sputtered.

After I cleared away all the hurt and pain and guilt I had held about my parents, I wrote them love letters loaded with forgiveness.

Dear Mother:

You know that I have struggled with my feelings about you and me since I was a youngster. I thought you were tough and I always wanted you to love me, and I don't think that you ever have. Throughout my childhood, more than anything, I wanted you to take joy in who I was and what I accomplished. I never felt that you did, until my perceptions of what happened changed.

Mother, please forgive me for being angry with you because you didn't show up when I won the spelling bee, or read a poem in the citywide contest, or was in a play, or made the National Honor Society. Someone pointed out to me that you were a single mother working five-and-a-half days a week to support six children. You were doing what you had to do. I saw you as a martyr when I should have seen you as a caring mother.

I accused you of being ashamed of me, when in truth I did not accept myself. Blaming you for my club feet and being short in stature has nearly destroyed me. When I labeled you self-righteous, I was describing my own worst defect of character. I was the drunk, not you. You co-signed loans and I never paid them, because I was trying to get back at you. Now I know that the circumstances God created for me were my opportunities to succeed with God's continuing guidance. But I left God and you in my wake.

I ask you to forgive me for how I harmed you. My amends will be to treat my life as God's business, not mine. When I see a chance to do for someone else I will, in your name.

I have a picture of you on my desk. When I look at it I whisper, "I love you, Mom."

Please forgive me,
Albert

I wrote my father a love letter as well. His was easier, because he and I are so alike. Writing his letter was similar to the letter I wrote myself.

Dear Dad:

It has been so much easier to blame you for all the bad that happened to me rather than to look at me. When I look at you, I see myself. I didn't have to walk away from six children to identify with you; I never had the courage to be unselfish enough to have a relationship where I could have children.

I want you to know that I love you. The humor I have comes from your gene pool; the ability to get along with anyone, rich or poor, was a quality you passed along to me as well. No one told a better story than you did, nor was better able to be a friend to someone—going to any lengths to make their life better. The greatest gift you passed along to me was laughter. As poor as we were growing up—even though you were an absentee parent—you could always see the slightest hint that dark clouds were about to open up to a sky full of possibilities.

But most of all I love you because loving you lets me love me. The one thing that I have always wanted (without knowing it) is self-love. There is nothing better than writing my soul twin to say through it all, "I love my Dad."

I love you,
Albert

Gosh, I still get a lump in my throat and become light-headed with wide-open spaces in my heart as I write and reread the letters I wrote to my parents. Nothing would have been possible—not Scott or Mrs. Hornblow or the Bells and most of all not the wonderful and life-giving clients I have worked with through the years—had I not repaired the rip in my heart and the disconnect with Mom and Dad.

Love is all there is.

CHAPTER 10

The End of the Journey

Nothing that is written on an occult tablet, like the Rosetta Stone, or hidden in a hope chest, like an Ark of the Covenant, will answer all life's questions. Certainly there's no flashing sign, "That's all folks!" to tell us when we've reached the end of the line on life's pilgrimage. There is always more—more lessons to learn and more people to love.

In going through all the ups and downs of life, hooking up with "isms" and dogmas (I call them bow-wows and loud barking) that attempt to capture us by offering us a master plan, it is our pain and suffering that will get us to where we need to go.

Rudyard Kipling's poem "If" has done more to keep

me on course, with its couplets of possibilities as well as caveats to beware of, than all the sermons I have preached or homilies I have shut out of my ears and head. Walt Whitman's *Leaves of Grass* has stirred me and moved me oftentimes through that valley of the shadow of death, so that like Ram Dass, I'm still here.

There are only two payouts in life—only two things through all the triumphs and failures you will have that will be written in a Lamb's Book of Life or in the hearts and souls of those who knew you: did he love and did he serve others?

I am asked constantly when does one get to the end of the rainbow and get to wallow in all the goodies that supreme effort to change promises. Unfortunately there is no fairy godmother with a wand that magically transforms us from frog to prince or from charwoman to princess. Let's pretend that Mother Goose and Grimm's Fairy Tales offer spiritual truths wrapped in fable. But we must be able to see the life lessons they offer, and improve our lot by the choices we make when certain situations present themselves.

SHARING THE STAGES

It was time for me to share the stages with someone dear to me.

Gloria, my recovery sponsor's wife, and I have known

one another since I got sober in 1980. I wanted to tell her what had happened to me. She was the one person I could say anything to who would remain open-minded.

She was the first speaker I heard when I entered recovery all those years ago. I will never forget that night when she said from the podium, "My name is Gloria and I'm an alcoholic. Tonight I feel clean inside, because I've gotten rid of all secrets and shame from my years of drinking and running with outlaws. If anybody in this meeting is looking for an easier, softer way, twelve-step sobriety is the best deal in town. This is the only way that worked for me."

Years later, Gloria and I met for dinner so I could explain my recent education.

"Gloria, I want to tell you all that I have found out about myself through meditation and a High Self consciousness," I said.

Through the long story about Paul and the stages, she didn't say a word. She listened, and I intuited that she believed me.

"I have lived thousands of lives, famous and infamous—both as a man and as a woman—some as a good little boy or girl, and a lot where I was a bad apple. I chose my parents and siblings because they provided the proper DNA, family dysfunctions, and also positive qualities that would best help me fulfill my destiny.

"I am not who you think I am, and neither are you. I chose alcoholism to help me tear down who I am not; I failed at life in order to rebuild from rack and ruin I have endured major struggles with my sexuality, because I needed to discover that my soul is both male and female. When I conquer the desire body, the soul man emerges. The desire body is how my ego has kept me trapped in an identity that was not mine.

"We have told one another since we met twenty-five years ago that we love the good life. You've remarked that we both like to sponsor newcomers trying to get sober. It's amazing how often my ego has swooped in to give me something that I think I want only to grow tired and depressed from the very thing I longed for. And it is just as painful to face what God takes away from me," I said.

Gloria's faith and trust in God were tested harshly when her oldest child, Bobby, sober for eight years after living on the streets, abusing heroin, and engaging in prostitution, died of AIDS in 1990. His passing was not a matter of slipping quietly through the veil into what we call death. It took weeks and weeks for Bobby to die. He suffered horribly. Gloria agonized. His sister Lisa sang and laughed with her brother until the end. They all cried and asked, "Why Bobby?"

After my dinner with Gloria, in 1991, we drove down the serpentine East Valley Road to the bookstore at the Sarada Convent. I bought a copy of Eknath Easwaran's *The End of Sorrow,* a commentary on the *Bhagavad Gita,* and handed it to Gloria.

"Just to make sure that there's no more unfinished business about Bobby, read this. You'll be freer than you've been since the day you got sober," I said.

"What is it about?"

"It is the story of how human beings, like Don Quixote, fight windmills, but our difficulties—the wars we wage—are of our own making. The book helps you to meditate and make peace within you. Read it, Gloria."

She and I strolled to the temple a few yards away and, after removing our shoes, walked in and sat down and began to meditate.

After half an hour, Gloria and I walked out together and took a side path flanked by oleander and cymbidium flower beds. We sat on the ground and looked up at the starry skies and out toward the Pacific Ocean. A full moon lit up the night.

"I feel clean inside. Remember when you said how clean you felt the first time I heard you speak, Gloria? God is finally helping me let go of the bondage of self and others. I see with new eyes," I said quietly.

"I feel quiet peace and tranquility. I came today with sadness and regret. The temple has a special energy. Were angels present in the temple, Albert?"

"Angels are everywhere, Gloria. You and I are not who we think we are. We are fallen angels rediscovering the power of God within ourselves."

"Bobby is an angel, I just know it. Angels wrapped

their wings around my son and took him to Paradise." Gloria's voice cracked with emotion as she spoke.

"Come over here under this tree. Let's meditate together. I am going to do something with you that I've never done. We are going to attempt to get Paul to speak through me about Bobby," I said to Gloria. We sat together beneath a spreading oak.

Within minutes we both were in a relaxed state. Through me Paul spoke aloud to Gloria:

You came here today, Gloria, looking for a sign.

"I am looking for a sign for what?" Gloria asked.

You want a sign that Bobby's soul is alive.

Crickets started evening anthems. Foghorns sounded from distant boats. In the moment, still minds and electric telepathy converged somewhere between Heaven and the mountaintop.

When you think thoughts that make you feel love, angels are in the field. As you clear away all blocks and barriers to your true identity, you activate angelic memory and draw the energies to you, from among yourselves, and from Paradise.

Walk in the light. Become one from within, where God is. Never start the journey back without a brother. Know that love is all there is, and you will identify with the angel you are.

Angels who restore and reclaim original progeny remain on Earth to rebuild the God connection.

Earth can be as Heaven when the souls of the angelic realm begin to grow in number.

When a pilgrim returns home through death, sickness, accident, or old age, his soul goes through a period of adjustment. There are no accidents. Every minute detail of a life is preordained.

Souls who come back must go through reform school and a vibration detoxification. As you must return with a brother or sister, spirit angels are in service to you and to others. When someone dies and returns to Heaven, he cannot communicate with you during his period of quarantine.

Do you have any questions?

Gloria still wanted to know if Bobby was alive in the afterlife and if he was happy.

Today in the Sarada bookstore, Albert gave you an angel as a sign.

There was silence but for the sound of the wind. Gloria swallowed and began to breathe rapidly, for her own intuition would not allow her to conceal her joy.

Gloria, someone wants to speak to you

And just as Paul had used my voice and my intelligence to speak with Gloria, Bobby spoke to his mother.

"I love you, Mom," a faint, soft voice spoke.

"I love you, Bobby."

SWAMI AND THE STAGES

The morning after I met with Gloria, I took a walk after breakfast with Swami in the high hills on Bella Vista.

"Swami, I know who I am. I know I'm not who every-body thinks I am. I'm not even who I thought I was. I'm a precious child of God who must bring my brother with me on my journey back to my authentic self," I spoke hurriedly.

"Ramapriya, I remember once when you came to me and said, 'Who am I?' To what do you owe this new awareness?" he asked.

I stopped on the road for a second.

"I got still enough to hear God when He spoke to me. Ramapriya became teachable enough to let go of the will of the ego and be who he has always been.

"There have been stages of this development, which started with my reconnecting to the light, the God source, the Divine, all of the fancy ways we refer to Om-nipotence," I said.

"Tell me about the ego. Is it a good thing or a bad thing, Ramapriya?"

"Not good or bad, but in need of being converted, much as a rabbi or priest or minister would an infidel."

"How did you convert it?" Swami asked.

"I loved it. I loved it until he and I were one and the same, a precious child of God. I could not be redeemed if I hated my ego. It is a big part of who I am, just mis-guided and Godless. I had to make my ego my best friend."

"Ramapriya, if the former ego self was Godless, how

did you include God or the Divine in your spiritual development and into selfhood?" my guru asked.

"I had to answer the question, God or no God?, and then stop debating the issue. Debate never got me anywhere, but faith has strengthened me and supported my errant behavior until the love of God could complete the conversion process through right use of will and concern for all mankind." I told him all this with the wide-eyed excitement of a child unwrapping his presents on Christmas morn.

"Swami, it is as if I woke from a nightmare or opened my eyes for the first time as to who I am and how this new awareness could change my life forever, one day at a time. I walked out of darkness and into the light of what the world was all about, how it was created and the purpose of coming back to earth—to become who I have always been though I didn't know it or act like it," I told him with a sense of sadness of reflection.

At this juncture in our walk, Swami wanted to sit quietly for a few minutes. He has told me often that he is pleased to be a teacher but often the struggles burden even a guru.

When we resumed on our journey, Swami's curiosity was piqued enough for our conversation to advance with more questions from him and answers from me.

I anxiously jumped right into explaining the next stage of soul refinement.

"Swami, Stage Four was as obvious as the nose on my

face but had become the proverbial 'elephant in the living room.' The reflection from the karmic mirrors of my family and friends and enemies caused me to remember that no one was doing anything to harm me; rather all the people and circumstances in my life that I perceived had made life more difficult for me were in fact reminders of the bad things I had done to other people. This stage helped me to stop playing the blame game and to claim what I have done in this life and past ones to damage another."

"When did you get so pious that you can excuse what others had done to harm you, Ramapriya?"

"You better than anyone know that the struggle that I have had with self-righteousness. I can only change me. I have no business trying to tell others what is wrong with them. Perhaps, one day each one who was a mirror for me to see what amends I needed to make for my bad-boy behavior may be able to look within themselves to change them," I answered.

"I suspect that you are getting closer to the Atman, the Brahmin inside you," Swami chuckled.

"Is your mind calm enough to tell me the true meaning of stage five, which says that you're not who you think you are, and there is little difference between a man and a woman? What does that mean to you and how did the stage awaken you?" he asked.

"Mistaken identity was a matter of being schooled by

people who didn't know who they were, and I chose the destructive behavior of alcoholism to lead me on an intuitive search for answers to who I really am.

"The real crux of identity is to be found in one's sexuality. None of us is really a man or a woman. We are both. We must embrace the androgyny of consciousness to be able to discover who we are. A child is born to correct lost soul conditions from prior lives that have perpetuated that child's false self. When we die, based upon what we have cleared and cleaned up of past transgressions, we can return to the perfect place where God lives."

"You seemed to have remembered a lot on your journey to clear away the wreckage of present and past lives. But what about the rest of stage five: you're not who you think you are?" Swami continued.

"No one has the key to who we are; rather our true self is revealed within us. The reason we cannot know true self is because our egotistical false self has played a game that has kept us from who we are. Mother sees us as her child and trains us in her ways according to her impressions of who we are and what we need to do with our lives. A lover sees us as what he needs us to be to fit his needs, his expectations. The church needs for us to be the sinner so its dogma can save us.

"The ego-created world of material illusion is created outside man. The illusionary world is an enemy to the angel that he is," I answered.

"You are speaking of the Atman, Ramapriya. And stage six?" he asked.

"The stage of forgive and forget-me-nots says that we must make amends to ourselves and others or we will not be able to let go of the wreckage of the past. Hurting oneself is as destructive as harming somebody else. It is the stage that frees us from all the dirt, guilt, and shame of past misdeeds. Through forgiveness we cut the umbilical cord to people, places, and things that are connected to the ledger of our miscreant self. Seek forgiveness, and that person or situation will never come back into your life with the same karma. Forgiveness changes how we relate to others, excluding former perceived enemies. And I love the fact that all the people from whom we seek forgiveness or who ask our forgiveness become unforgettable because they too are touchstones to our soul growth," I said.

"Continue with seven and eight. I need to hear while you are so clear," Swami cajoled me with his humor.

"Stage seven says that you must bring your brother to the light. This one stumped me for a while because I thought that this implied that we are our brother's keeper, which, to me, was archaic Old Testament truth that was outmoded because of the birth, life, death, and resurrection of Christ consciousness," I said.

"Your problem, Ramapriya, is that you confuse God's truth with man's heresy. Now give me the clear answer, please," he requested.

I never feel shamed by Swami, only amended to better understanding.

"We are all interconnected and interrelated. Each of us returns to Earth one by one, but we are able to find our way home in twos or more. The ancient teachings caution us to share what we receive—to love thy brother as thyself—never to receive for the self alone. The road home requires that we come back with someone lost and confused, who represents the dark side of ourselves. We project our shadow selves onto our enemies, who teach us more than our friends. Love and embrace your shadow, recognize it as the dark part of God—the Great Deceiver—and convert it with love, and you will be who you really are.

"Stage eight says that love is the Great Redeemer, God's glue that holds His fallen angels together as they help one another—with no payoff and no motive but to let the God within us love his fellowman," I said.

Squirrels scampered and dogs barked, and we continued to walk together in silence. The teacher said nothing, and the student began to learn that not all correct responses would be rewarded with praise.

Swami spoke again.

"I have changed my mind about where you should live and where you should work. If it is still your pleasure, you may come here to Montecito and live at the monastery. You will be of great assistance to our caretaker, Anadi."

A long time ago I asked my guru if I could move to the grounds of the Sarada Convent, my favorite place in the world. I wanted to build a house and live there until I died. Back then, he said, "Stay where you are."

I sat down in the middle of the road, cupping my face in my hands. Then I jumped up and hopped around like the little kid I used to be that I had just rescued from his rat hole of shame.

"No. No. No. No, Swami. Don't you see? I don't need to hide out at the monastery here in Montecito. I know what I am supposed to do. I know my purpose. God is working through me. When the client comes to me, he comes as me. When the client heals, I heal. With your blessing, I will continue to see God in all my clients. God touches me every single day, even when I do not know He is reaching out to me. But as you said, 'See God in others long enough and God will reach out and touch you.' Well, He has and He does, through the clients who counsel with me," I proffered.

Swami smiled and we continued to walk.

"Well, since you won't make me tea and listen to my lectures in the temple or comfort the devotees when they come, perhaps it is best for you to remain in Sedona as long as it is God's will. You once said to me that God does not care where you work and where you live; He cares how you work and how you live," Swami said.

After we walked a few more steps, my teacher said,

"For now, Ramapriya, I think I want to take that turn there." He pointed to a right-turn dirt-road intersection.

"God wants to show you something on a road you have never traveled. Are you willing?"

He was walking faster, and I hastened to catch up, chattering excitedly.

"Swami," I cried out as I picked up pace, "I have one last question. Paul says that all of us are trying to go home. He talks about Heaven. Just where is Heaven?"

He stopped and turned to me with a big grin on his face.

"All this time you are gathering lessons that will take you and others to Heaven and you don't know where you are going?" Swami laughed loudly and his merriment caused tears of joy to run down his cheeks.

"Aha ha, ha ha, Ramapriya, you are so amusing and amazing. The kingdom of Heaven is quite near to you."

With a long brown finger he tapped on my chest. "The kingdom of Heaven is within," he said calmly.

For a moment or two neither of us moved. Our eyes involuntarily closed, and we began to breathe in and breathe out. Silent and still on the dusty road, my teacher led me through Heaven's gate. I was home. The search for Paradise was over. Then Swami Swahananda set off at a brisk pace. I stood where I was. As I came back to the present, I realized that once again the teacher was far ahead of the student.

I raced after him, shouting.

"Swami, the most incredible thing happened last evening. My friend Gloria spoke with her son Bobby, who is an angel in Heaven, and you wouldn't believe . . ."

And the wise man and the fool trudged the winding back roads of God's panorama, speaking of cabbages and kings and hills that God built for man to climb. A large band of angels walked with these pilgrims to keep them company in the beautiful verdant mountains of Montecito.

Author's Note

It is my hope that you will experience the great awakening in your life that I did in mine and that the eight life stages that were given to me may be of benefit to you. I would encourage you to seek divine guidance from your High Self as I did with mine. Do not be discouraged when you intuitively call the name of your spiritual guide and he does not answer on the first or second try. Be patient and ask often for help with your life's purpose. There are no calendars or clocks to announce when that moment of deep and abiding connection to a power greater than yourself will click for you. This is the promise: God will speak to you when you pray and you will hear his answers if you listen.

May God bless you and keep you as you interconnect and interrelate with all your brothers and sisters along your spiritual path.

And never forget that love is all there is.

Appendix

Lunar and Solar Eclipses

2006
9/7 lunar eclipse: 15 degrees of Pisces
9/22 solar eclipse: 29 degrees of Virgo

2007
3/3 lunar eclipse: 12 degrees of Virgo
3/19 solar eclipse: 28 degrees of Pisces
8/12 solar eclipse: 19 degrees of Leo
8/28 lunar eclipse: 4 degrees of Pisces

2008
2/7 solar eclipse: 17 degrees of Aquarius
2/21 lunar eclipse: 1 degrees of Virgo
8/1 solar eclipse: 9 degrees of Leo
8/16 lunar eclipse: 24 degrees of Aquarius

2009

2/9 lunar eclipse: 20 degrees of Leo

2/15 solar eclipse: 6 degrees of Pisces

7/7 lunar eclipse: 15 degrees of Capricorn

7/22 solar eclipse: 29 degrees of Cancer

8/6 lunar eclipse: 13 degrees of Aquarius

8/20 solar eclipse: 27 degrees of Leo

12/16 lunar eclipse: 24 degrees of Sagittarius

12/31 solar eclipse: 10 degrees of Cancer

2010

6/12 solar eclipse: 21 degrees of Gemini

6/26 lunar eclipse: 4 degrees of Capricorn

12/5 solar eclipse: 13 degrees of Sagittarius

12/21 lunar eclipse: 29 degrees of Gemini

2011

6/1 solar eclipse: 11 degrees of Gemini

6/15 lunar eclipse: 24 degrees of Sagittarius

12/10 lunar eclipse: 18 degrees of Gemini

12/14 solar eclipse: 2 degrees of Capricorn

2012

6/4 lunar eclipse: 14 degrees of Sagittarius

6/19 solar eclipse: 28 degrees of Gemini

11/13 solar eclipse: 21 degrees of Scorpio

11/28 lunar eclipse: 6 degrees of Gemini

ACKNOWLEDGMENTS

First and foremost I want to thank Karin Price Mueller for her brilliant edit of this book. Karin "got" the book from the first page and made its message clearer and more accessible. To the team at Atria Books, from publisher Judith Curr, whom I respect and admire for her prescience about books that the public needs to read; to Johanna Castillo, with no-nonsense but fair and balanced eyes; Amy Tannenbaum, sweet and adorable with a minesweep intelligence, and all those in promotion and advertising who have done a lot to make this book a success, a big resounding "thank you."

I want to thank Gail, David, Ashley, and Andrew Bell for your friendship and encouragement; you are First Family for me.

To consciousness-raising James and Salle Merrill-

Redfield, there are not enough words to express my thanks to you both for all the years of friendship and support of Scott and me and the work we do.

For spiritual guidance and friendship, I want to thank my soul sisters, the nuns at the Sarada Convent in Santa Barbara, California.

And foremost to my spiritual teacher, Swami Swahananda of the Vedanta Society of Southern California, I am humbled by your willingness to be a part of this book and grateful to you for steering me in the right direction when I lost my way.

I want to thank my brothers and sisters, Mary, Bill, Henry, Jeannie, and Margie, and especially my parents, for allowing me to be true to myself.

Always I am thankful for the Sedona Intensive support team. Without you there would be no clear and conscious program.

I want to acknowledge my Saturday-morning sober group for keeping me sane and sober. You are my lifeline.

And to every single client who ever went through the Sedona Intensive, I thank you for my clearing.

I want to give my heartfelt thanks to Dorothy Wood Espiau for being such a good friend and a positive force in my life.

I would be remiss if I forgot the late and great darling Leonora Hornblow, my muse and dearest friend for more than twenty years. Who I have become I attribute to your wise counsel.

I thank you, Paulo Coelho, and your tuning fork a million times over for awakening all of us who are warriors of the light to our mission in the world. God bless you and your masterpiece, *The Alchemist*, which helped me discover the Santiago within me.

And most of all to my business partner and best friend Scott Carney, thank you for your love and support and for helping me to become who I really am.